SURVIVED

by

FAITH

and

GRACE

Carolyn Collett

ISBN 978-1-63814-045-0 (Paperback)
ISBN 978-1-63814-046-7 (Hardcover)
ISBN 978-1-63814-047-4 (Digital)

Covenant Books, Inc.
11661 Hwy 707
Murrells Inlet, SC 29576
www.covenantbooks.com

To my daughters, Tonya and Cindy, so they know the strength they come from and will never doubt the love that I have for them.

To my husband, John, for the love and devotion he has given me through my life since I was sixteen years old.

To my grandkids, who will know the love I had for them and the joy they, as well as their mom's, brought to my life, and that bullying is a cowardly act of insecurity. Stay true to yourselves and know the power of God's grace in their lives.

This is about telling my story of hardships, sadness, worry, heartaches, and happiness. I was the tenth child of my mother and father. They had already gotten most of their children grown, five boys and four girls and a granddaughter and another grandchild on the way. My father had worked in the coal mines in the early years for a dollar a day with their first five children. My older brothers and sisters would tell me stories about the life they had, and only one of them graduated high school. A few of them didn't even finish grade school. Two brothers said they had to leave school in sixth grade and get jobs. I was told my father would spend his wages in the bars and honky-tonks, beers, and women.

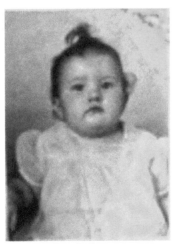

my first baby picture

He got his back broke in the mines and had to find another job, and there were no other jobs except coal mines, and he had to go away from home in Ohio and find a job with other locals who were unable to work in the coal mines anymore. After that, he only came home on occasion. My mom had five more children, and my father came home less and less during that time, making it very difficult for my mother. She had to raise all the kids by herself.

I was also told by my older brothers that when he was not away at work, he was still never at home much for our family. My mother went on to have four more children during this time while he was coming and going back and forth to Ohio. Then when her baby boy was around five years old, another surprise happened, and that was me. When I was born, my grandmother Cindy came to stay with my mom. She died soon after, but she was the one who named me. My mom said she was the finest woman she had ever known as I grew up. She said she was blessed to have her as a mother.

my Mom and her Mother

I was born in the old red siding house up far in a hollow where we would live for a few years. The neighbor lady delivered me. Someone later said she was a midwife, but I didn't think she was, and she had said my dad was not home, and it took another eight days after my birth for the doctor to get there and ensure everything was okay with my mom and me. I was the fifth girl and the last baby for my mom and dad.

My mom was forty-five years of age, and my dad was fifty-three. No, it did not make me special like one would think. Was I in for a complete surprise so my story goes? Growing up, I never felt like I had a stable loving home. It was always going from one place to another moving here and there. It was never like my home anywhere I was and maybe because I was not in one place very long.

My first memory goes back to when I was about two and a half years old. I could not talk yet, just in my mind, but I knew what was happening around me. If I wanted something or attention from someone, I was a pointer and a grunter.

My mother left me in the care with my two older sisters, Lou and Patty, and I remember when she advised them to watch me closely to make sure I did not get hurt and especially keep me away from the porch. Our porch was about a foot and a half off the ground with no railing. So there was nothing to hold me in, and I was a chubby little thing and could barely walk. Sure enough, off the porch I went. Of course, they were not worried because up to that time, I had not tried to talk, and they said mommy would never know. I didn't have any bruises, and no one would have to know of the accident. However, when she arrived home, I went out the walkway to meet her and pointed to my head and to the porch, making some sounds which told her I fell off the porch.

She knew immediately that my big sisters had taken their eyes off me and let me fall. I am sure they got into some trouble. It was a few years later before she allowed them to babysit me again.

Our house was an old red siding four-room place that was cold we had two places to make a fire one when you went in the front door, and on the other side was the bedroom and another fireplace. I remember the smell of the ashes and the coal brought in buckets to start the fire. I slept with my mom always, and I remember I would wake up, and she would not be there. I didn't know where she would be; I felt scared and alone. I would just lie there and cry myself back to sleep while wondering if she would be coming back. The only time this happened was when my dad came in for a visit. I realized, when I grew up, the reason for the disappearances at night. I thought of my poor mom. What a life she did live.

me at 3 years old

At age three, we moved to Morrow, Ohio. We didn't live there, but about a year, we had a big water pond on the property there, and my two older brothers, Matt and Zach, would sneak off and get in the pond to swim. My mom would be scared they might drown, and that I would try and follow them, so we moved back to Kentucky. She, at that time, still had five kids at home to look after. I wish we would have stayed there, for I am sure that the boys would not have drowned. I knew the Lord had to be looking after us. We had to move back in the hollow in the red siding house because of them. I did not like that house and had a fear inside me when I was there. It was a very sad time for me, and I cried often. The house had an uneasy unloving feel to it. Very hard to explain other than saying it was not a happy place.

I was about four when Zach taught me how to ride a bike. He would just put me on and said, "Ride or go over that big hill." So I made a good choice; I didn't go over the hill. I learned to ride the bike and wondered what he would have done if I had wrecked and went in the creek. He had faith in me. He was a good big brother.

Another story around that time, there was a row of warts on my hand going up my finger. There must have been seven or eight.

The other kids would make fun of them, asking, "What are those things on your hand?"

I was just a little girl; I did not know why they were there. But thanks to my mom, I remember her counting them, and she took me outside. We gathered up the number of warts with little rocks, and she had a cloth—may had been a handkerchief—and placed the rocks in it and tied it together. We walked, holding my hand up the steep hill at our little red siding house, and placed the cloth filled with rocks on the top, and she said to me, "Now all your warts will go away," and they did the next few days, and I had no scars at all.

I still think a lot about that because I hated those warts and was so happy when they disappeared and never came back. My mom could do anything in my mind. She didn't usually show me a lot of love, but that was okay. I knew she had a hard life and a bunch of other kids and not much help from her husband.

my Mom

There was a path going to my oldest sister Jean's house. She had a little girl. Her name was Jenny. She was two years older than me and a little boy Noah who was three years younger than me, and I loved them both so much and liked to play with. So I would go up that path to get to her house. I would climb the steep steps to their house and knock on the door. If my sister was having a good day, she would let me in to play, but if not, she would give me a very stern look, and I would run back down the steps and on the path home. My sister Jean had five children and worked very hard for her family. She was always a loving fine woman who put her kids first. I loved her and Brian, her husband. He was always so good to me and a good humble man. Jenny and Noah were my best friends, and later in the day, Jenny would come down the path, and we would play. I never had anyone else to play with during this time in my life.

When I was four years old, my dad was home from working away in Ohio. I was playing as no one was there except me, my mom, and my uncle Henry who lived with us. The other kids were in school. I went into the bedroom and saw my dad on top of my mom. I screamed out to get him off my mom and ran over to get him off as fast as I could at four years old, and I was screaming loud crying, and he yelled very loudly with a mean voice back and told me to get out. I cried and was so scared for my mom. I went running to my uncle and told him to go and get my mommy because my daddy was on top of her, and I was sure she was crying. He told me to go outside and play and be quiet.

little coal bucket

He gave me a little bucket and told me to go put some pieces of coal in it for him to put on the fire. I did that and felt fear around my daddy thereafter because I was so afraid of him. I did not understand why he was hurting my mommy. No one ever told me that was a normal thing between a husband and wife. My mom never tried to explain to me that was okay. He was not trying to hurt her. She never picked me up and gave me a hug for comfort and assurance that she was okay. My dad did not even look at me. My thoughts of him consisted of he was mean and scary. This stayed with me until he passed away. He never showed me anything to change these feeling about him.

Once again, my mom left me with Lou and Patty, and they had boyfriends who wanted to take them somewhere, and I said no Patty was about 15 years old and Lou was about 13, these guys were brothers. I was not going anywhere with them. I had made up my mind when Patty's boyfriend said, "I will give you fifty cents to go," and they begged, so I agreed. When we got in the car, I didn't like it. We had a long road to get out of our hollow. He had given me the fifty-cent piece, and I was holding tight in my little hand. We got to the bridge at the mouth of the hollow, and I told them I wanted to go back home. My sisters assured me I would be okay, and we were going, so I started to cry and told them I was telling them to mommy that I was scared and wanted to go home, so they turned around, and we went back up the hollow to our house.

The man said, "Give me back that fifty cents."

I said no and ran in the house. Lou and Patty were so mad at me.

Life was not good growing up those first four and a half years living up in that hollow. The graveyard was right on the top of the hill. I was scared to go by it, and there were huge coal trucks that went up and down the road every day that was also very scary to me. We moved to Ohio again, and I was so happy somehow. I knew I was not supposed to live in a place like this even at that age. I knew there was so much more, and I was ready to find it.

I had turned five years old, and up to then, I had not experienced many good things other than playing with Jenny and Noah from time to time. I'm sure my sisters, Lou and Patty, love me, but I must have been in their way of having fun with boyfriends. My brothers, Matt and Zach, were both good brothers to me and would watch over me as best they could.

We moved to a big house that had a bathroom inside and was much different from our little red siding house back home. This was the second move for us to Ohio in less than two years. I started first grade at Price Elementary School in Amelia, Ohio. When I was five years old, I was a happy kid full of excitement to start in the big school and have lots of friends, or so I thought.

my first grade school

I had one friend in first grade; his name was Tuffy. That could have been a nickname, but that was the only name I knew. He lived across the road from me, and we played together often. I had such a hard time fitting in school. The kids would laugh at me and call me a hillbilly. Of course, I didn't know what that name meant, and no one wanted to play with me, and the teacher showed me no empathy. She was not a nice person at all, and no one ever asked me about how my day at school was when I got home.

There was really nothing wrong with me. I was a normal kind of cute little girl who played nice when I got the chance. It was a very hard struggle trying to get these kids to play with me. They would just stare and act as they had never seen anyone like me. They all—I thought—looked just like me, just kids. I think maybe it was my clothes; I didn't have any other than the hand-me-downs from Jenny, and she was seven now, and I got what I had mostly from her. I like them all just fine; I didn't see anything wrong with how I looked or dressed.

One day, the assignment was that each student had to go up to the front with the teacher and point out what they had for breakfast that morning on the food pyramid, and as I was watching the other students point out what they had with the yardstick, I did not see anything on there that I had ever had for breakfast or any other meal for that matter. I was scared because I did not know what would happen when it was my turn.

Finally, my name was called, and slowly I made my way to the front beside the teacher. I was hoping she would be nice to me this day. She asked me to point the foods that I had eaten that morning for breakfast, and I just stood there as I did not see chocolate gravy and biscuits as they were not on there. She asked me to look at her, and I did.

She said, "What is wrong with you?"

I said nothing, and she said, "Why then are you not showing the class what you had for breakfast?"

I looked at her and said, "Because there is nothing on here that I had for breakfast," and the kids all were laughing at me.

She said, "Well then, you just tell the class and me what you had."

With a nervous voice, I said, "I had biscuits and chocolate."

my first grade picture

Then she let out a sigh, and the kids laughed even louder and were talking among themselves. I couldn't figure out what I had done and why they were laughing at me. The teacher very sternly told me to sit down. She had never heard of anything like that. I was sure she and all the kids in that class did not like me. I felt sad and very alone. But little did I know, things would get much worse.

I just somehow knew and hoped things would get better for me at this school, and I would have friends. I had struggled to make friends, and I was nice to everyone, but no one wanted to play with me. The only friend I had was Tuffy. We would play in the evening when we got home from school, and that was fun. Christmas time came, and all the students were to bring a gift to exchange. I was excited as I had never gotten a Christmas gift before. We only got a brown bag with an apple and orange and a few pieces of candy in it every Christmas unless my aunt Ethel sent us something.

The day came; I finally had something to look forward to.

My mom had given me a little gift wrapped in brown paper, and I was happy to take it, so we all got seated. The presents were taken to the front desk of the teacher. She would call a name, and you would go get your present. As my name was called, I almost ran up and got this most beautiful present. I had never seen anything like it.

I got back to my desk and unwrapped the gift, and there it was—a huge box of crayons and a huge coloring book. It's the best thing a little girl could ever dream of getting. I had never felt so happy in my life.

About the time I was opening the crayons, I heard a little girl cry out said, "This is no fair! Who would bring this as a present?"

I looked up, and the teacher was standing over me and jerked the crayons and the coloring book out of my hand, and she said, "You brought this?"

I said, "I don't know because I didn't know what was in that brown paper."

She had a very mean look on her face, and she threw down the small box of cherry candy and said, "How dare you bring something like this to our Christmas party! You keep it and eat it. You are not included in our gift exchange."

my mom and dad

She gave my crayons and coloring book to that other kid, and all the kids laughed at me. I just sat there and cried. I am sure my mom could not afford to buy a gift but wanted me to have something to take. I never got another present like that again during my childhood years. Just a coloring book and a big box of crayons, but to me, it was the most wonderful present in the world. Such simple things can make a difference. After that day, nothing was ever the same. I knew my chances of making friends were done, so I did the best I could, and that teacher hardly even looked at me anymore.

My hair was long and pretty; my mom always kept it in braids with big ribbons. One evening, riding home on the bus, the little boy sitting behind me was pulling my hair, and I would tell him to stop and that it hurt me, but he would not stop. He kept pulling even harder and harder. I started to cry like no one was there to protect me. Matt and Zach went to the same school. They were in sixth and eighth grade and rode a different bus, and Lou and Patty were in high school.

So as I was getting off the bus, the driver said with a very hard look on his face, "What is wrong with you? Why are you crying?"

I said, "That little boy pulled my hair hard and would not stop. I am going to tell my mommy about him."

He looked very mad and slapped me right in the face hard and said, "You will tell no one." He pulled my hair and said, "You will not tell anyone I just slapped you, or you will be in big trouble and not ride my bus again."

Tears were streaming down my face as I got off the bus.

Tuffy said, "Are you okay?"

I said, "No, I don't want to go back to that school."

"It will be all right. I will be there to protect you. I am going to tell my mom. She will do something about this."

"Oh no, that bus driver will be sure to get me."

It was another sad day for this five-year-old little girl. My mom did not even notice I had been crying, and my face was red. I guess she had more things to think about that day. Somehow, I always felt my mom was not having any fun. She seemed to be busy working and cooking all the time. She never hugged me or told me she loved me, not once, and none of the family ever did. It seemed our family was not in rhythm with each other.

I would see Tuffy's mom welcome him home from school. Sometimes she would be at the bus waiting although it stopped right in front of our house. I sure wish she had been there the day that bus driver slapped my face.

One afternoon, my niece Jenny took me for a walk down on the highway, and she was seven years old holding tightly to my hand as cars went speeding. By then, there was a big white car with an older man stopped and said he wanted to give us a ride and to get in.

Jenny said "oh no" as she tightened her hand to mine. She said, "My uncle is standing right over there, watching us."

I said, "No, he's not."

She said, "Shhh."

We kept walking very fast, and he slowly was beside us and said, "I don't see anyone."

She said, "Well, he is right down there. Do you think two little girls would be out alone?" And right then, she yelled out, "Uncle Darrell, we are coming! This man wants us to get in his car."

The man sped away quickly, and we never went for another walk on that highway.

That always impressed me growing up like who would have known that a seven-year-old child could be so smart and protective at the same time. She was like an adult in a kid's body. I never knew why we went walking down that road and why our parents allowed us to go. Maybe they did not know we had left.

Matt, Zack, Jenny and me

My fifth year of life was hard. However, looking back, I learned a valuable lesson. You are a little tougher at any age than you realize. Faith comes when you don't yet know what it means. Somehow, we made it through the year, and I passed the first grade maybe because the teacher wanted to get rid of me, and my dad moved us back to our home in Kentucky, and I never knew why no one ever said. I think he may have gotten tired of having his family with him all the time.

I remember, pulling out in the big moving truck, I cried as Tuffy was waving bye to me. I never saw Tuffy again, and my little heart felt broken. So now we are back in Kentucky, and we have moved from our red siding house far up in the hollow to a white house at the mouth of the hollow, and the school was right beside across the road. This was where I started second grade at six years of age, and was I in for yet another surprise? No, this year was no better than the first grade. I was not used to having any friends, only Tuffy. My hair was still long and with lots of ribbons and bows. It was strange that my mom would take time to braid my hair and put lots of ribbons and bows but not hug me or hold me on her lap.

my 2nd grade school

My first day of school at the big two-room schoolhouse, which was also used as a church on Sunday, was damp and cold and smelled bad, not anything like my school in Ohio. Matt and Zach walked me to my seat and left, going over to the big room as it was called. One brother was in the sixth grade, and the other in the eighth grade called the big room, and first through fourth was called the little room. The room had a stove that had pipes going to the ceiling and was warm as coal was put in throughout the days to keep the rooms warm.

One teacher taught the little room, and one teacher taught the big room. I was hoping I would have a good person. However, it turned out she wasn't so nice after all. The kids I did not know said I talk funny, and about a day in the bullying began, we were outside playing when two of the girls each grabbed a pigtail of my hair and said, "Giddy up" like I was a horse or pony and marched me all around the schoolhouse. As they tore out my ribbons, I started to cry as this was hurting me so bad. I did not like my hair to be pulled. It took me back to the school bus in Ohio with the little boy pulling my hair. I never tried to fight back. I never wanted to fight or thought about hurting someone.

They were not nice at all and wanted to hurt me for a reason unknown to me because I did not know any of them. I tried hard to fit in, even making progress, talking like them with a southern slang, but nothing helped. That southern slang stayed with me. Some of the kids were just bullies. My mom would pack my lunch; she would put a pint of cow's milk in a jar with a lid, and sometimes a sandwich was my lunch. I remember one day, a kid had some peanut butter and crackers and offered me one. It was the best thing I had ever tasted. I was six years old and never tasted peanut butter and crackers. We had a hard time, but I didn't know it. Not having what other people had never bothered me, I guess.

My mom bought fresh milk off a lady up the road. We would walk through a pasture to get a gallon jug. There was a big bull that roamed the pasture, and she would tell me to be very quiet, and I could tell she was very afraid and scared of that bull, and we would always walk by the creek. Sometimes she would get cheese and homemade butter from the nice lady. She would make it last if she could, and then we would go back and get the same things. Sometimes she would only get milk. I would wonder why I had to be the one to go with her. She had two older sons who was eleven and thirteen.

my 2nd grade picture

My aunt Ethel came to visit us and brought me a little red-beaded purse. It was the prettiest purse in the world, I thought. So I carried it with me all the time, feeling ten feet tall and so pretty.

Looking for anything to put in it, I had two marbles, but I was stepping high with my purse in my hand. One day, an older student—as class was dismissing—ran up beside me on the road and jerked my purse out of my hand and threw it down and stomped on it. I was speechless, thinking, *Why is she doing this?*

I started to cry, and then she picked it up and threw it over in the creek that went down behind the school and just looked at me and laughed said, "Now what do you think about your pretty red purse?"

I couldn't do anything but stand there and cry, and then she called me a baby. I was crushed, not knowing why someone would do such a thing. I could never forget that day.

I felt so very sad. Why were so many of these students so mean to me? I was not doing anything to anyone. Zach got into a fight with her brother over this as he was so mad at her for doing this to me, but there was nothing he could do to her. He was a good brother. Much later in life, the girl who did this called me and apologized and said the reason she did it was she was jealous of me and wanted that purse and didn't want me to have it. I accepted the apology, and I love her to this day.

My mom didn't care much for any of the kids who lived in the hollow. She would slam the door when they come to ask me to play. I would be sad because I had no one to play with, and even with all the bullying, I still wanted to play, but Mommy would not allow. Sometimes if she went into town and I stayed home with my brothers, I would get to play outside, and it would make me happy just to have someone to play with. I came home every day with my hair all messed up, my ribbons and bows floating down the creek. I guess it was just too much for her.

As time went on, the bullying was more tolerable, and I was used to it. I tried to learn. I was very good with reading and writing. I always got one hundred for my writing. I was very good. My dad would work away in Ohio. It was just Matt, Zach, and me with our mom. She and I would go to the little store and get things we needed, and she would call the man who would deliver groceries to the house and get enough to last a month. She took good care of us.

I was not unhappy when the second grade ended. I was growing up in my little mind, and that was good. I felt very lucky to survive that grade, but with all the bullying, I guess it was a little better than first grade, and I had summer to look forward to. In the summer, my mom and I would go visit my dad in Ohio and stay in his apartment. It was dark with very little light it seemed, and I didn't like it there, but the milkman would drop off jars of milk, white and chocolate. I loved chocolate milk. I had never had any, and it was so good. The white milk did not taste like the milk from the nice lady's house that my mom and I walked through the pasture to get, which was so good. One would think this was not a big deal, but it was to me.

Then we would go back home on a Greyhound bus, and my dad would stay there. I didn't get to play much during the summer while school was out, only with my niece or nephews. My mom was very strict. Kids in the hollow would get to go swimming in the creek and swing on grapevines, but doing these great things came much later for me.

Fall came, and it was time to start third grade. They were building a big brand-new school. Everyone was so excited. However, we went to the old school across the road for a couple of months while they were finishing to get the opening ready, and the worst thing that could happen, well, happened. I got licks with a paddle from the teacher. It was one of the worst days of my life. For each math problem, we got wrong was one lick, and I missed ten. I did not have much time to study the questions, and I, of course, didn't have anyone to help me study, but I did not expect to get a paddling in the third grade, but I wasn't the only one who got the paddle. There were several students who got worse than me. It was not a good day. I did not like that teacher at all, and it was just the beginning.

We finally got to move to our new school. I was happy and excited. I was sure that third grade would be my best year ever. We had a huge cafeteria to eat our lunch and a huge playground to play on with swings, slides, and seesaws. Life was good. The kids were better, not great. We had so many more kids there who came from different areas. I got a short break from bullying as they had so many to choose from. It didn't last long enough however before the hair-pulling and ribbons kept coming out. I guess my mom had enough and took me to the beauty shop. The lady pulled my hair up in a ponytail on my head and took scissors and cut off that ponytail. Well, I was in complete shock. My hair was awful. I cried and cried. I would rather have my head hurt and my hair pulled than to have this happen to me. It simply traumatized me for that entire year.

I wore a headscarf for weeks, and that only gave the kids more to laugh about and make fun of me. I hated my hair and hated school. Nothing seemed to be going right for me. Finally, it got tamed down, and I took off the scarf and got used to having very short hair. At least no one ever pulled my hair again maybe there was not enough to grab. Christmas came, and again I didn't participate anymore at school. My mom just kept me home because I had no gift to take and exchange. We didn't get gifts, only a little brown bag with an orange, apple, and couple pieces of candy, but it was all I needed, and I was thankful. I think these bags came from a local church and handed out for the kids in poor families.

Summertime came, and again we went to visit my dad on a big Greyhound bus, and I got sick and threw up on the bus, and the bus driver got so mad, but my mom stood up for me and settled him down. I guess I really didn't like to go visit my dad. Sometimes they would leave me in the room by myself when we got there, and I would wonder if either of them would come back. My dad never showed any emotion to me when we come in or when we left. It was like I was an invisible child. I was always ready to leave and go home.

my aunt Ethel and me

We also went that summer to see my aunt Ethel, the one who gave me the little red-beaded purse. She was so rich I thought she owned a restaurant in the big city. We would go there, and I would watch her work, and she always made me a dish of ice cream. She sure was a beautiful lady. I was a happy little kid when I was with her.

I would go to the bank with her, and I told her what happened with my red-beaded purse.

She said, "That wasn't your fault, and I will find you another one," and she did. She would fill the new purse with a roll of pennies and a roll of dimes. This was the best feeling in the world to be walking to the bank with her, holding my hand, and feeling loved for the first time in my life. I knew I had to leave, so I just enjoyed every minute I had with her. My cousin would come over; she also lived in the big city and had a supervisor job at the hospital. She was very beautiful, and I loved them both so much, and they loved my mom and me. I will write more about them both throughout my story.

The fourth grade was fast approaching, and the eight and nine years were coming. The first day arrived, and we met our teachers. All of them were still old to me; however, when you are nine years old, everyone who's grown up seems old. I really was excited thinking this was going to be my best year. It just had to get better. I was the best kid in class, or that's what I thought. I was not a bully, was nice to everyone, and just wanted to have a friend like Tuffy, but it was not happening for me. This year went smoothly, except at home. Zach was getting ready to quit school. He did not like it, and he was a junior, not long before he would be out. That was the talk I had heard.

Since my dad had retired, Zach and Matt had been different, but they still watched after me and were good brothers. We all had to walk to a bus stop at the top of the hill to catch our bus to school. I got my first whipping from my mom in fourth grade. It had been raining, and the roads were muddy as all the roads where we lived had not been upgraded to the blacktop.

One morning, the bus did not run, so the kids decided to walk down to the school. My brother, next to me, was in high school also, and his bus had not run either, and he was happy he did not have to go to school.

We started to walk, and he went back home and told my mom. She sent him back after me. We had gotten down the road on our way when I heard him call my name, and I had to go back. My mom was standing by the bridge with a big long switch. I had on a little skirt with knee socks, and she reached down, pushed those socks down, and whipped my legs all the way home with that switch and said, "Now try to walk to school again in the mud."

I didn't understand. I thought I was doing something good walking to school. However, she thought differently. I never walked to school again from that place we lived, and I have never forgotten that day.

One day, the family was all in. Everyone was sitting on the front porch, and Jenny and I were playing badminton as this was a game I loved and was good at, so we were entertaining the family, and as I went back to hit high, I fell backward in my mom's rosebush, and it tore my white blouse to shreds down my back, and I was bleeding, and it hurt me bad as it was full of thorns.

My mom yelled out and said, "You have destroyed my roses!" and

No one came over to try and help get me out of the thorns, and they were all laughing like it was funny. I was just a child hurt, and no one cared. I got myself up, went behind the house, and cried like a baby. I really think it hurt me more than I had ruined my pretty white blouse more than the thorns hurt. Nothing was ever said about it.

Noah

I loved to play with Jenny. She was older and wanted to play with the older girls, so her little brother, Noah, was a little younger than me, but we became best friends. We would play and never fight or argue; we were inseparable. We would find places to make playhouses and make places to slide down the hills. We made the best slide ever, going down the graveyard hill of all places where I was so afraid of when I was younger, and we would swing on grapevines from his house. In the graveyard one day, there were several kids swinging, including my brother Zach, and he would take more turns than he was supposed to and would get in front of all the rest of the kids. When it came to my turn, he jumped in front of me and said, "I am going," so he did, and when he swung out, the grapevine broke, and he fell hard to the ground, and I started to cry and was very scared if he was going to die, but he was okay. He got a broken arm, and I was sad for him but glad he took my place. That old grapevine was worn out.

He had to wear a cast on his arm for a long time it seemed. I don't think he ever swung on another grapevine, but we sure did.

creek where Noah and I used a car hood for a boat

My nephew Noah and I would build a swimming pool in the creek. There was nothing we could not think of to do. We would build playhouses and make a slide down the mountains, we had a big car hood, we would row down the creek whether it was clear or muddy water, we did not care, and we just liked to play and have lots of fun. Our car hood was taken away when we were trying to move it through some rocks. Noah cut his toe almost off on a broken bottle and had to be rushed to the hospital. I had never been so scared, but he was okay and was the last of our boat. We would have got into some trouble, but my sister was so happy. Noah was okay. We were saved from a whipping. However, we no longer had our car hood boat and had to learn to play other things, and we always did.

My dad brought home a little black-and-white puppy one evening, and I loved it. Immediately it was love at first sight of this puppy. We had a big dog named Rex, but he was not really a play dog, so I was excited about this puppy. He told me I could have it but would have to take care of it.

I said, "Oh yes, I will thank you."

A couple of weeks went by, and I was so attached I could hardly leave him for a minute. One day, I heard him squealing loudly and barking, so ran outside, and my dad was already heading toward the puppy. He got into a yellowjacket nest, and they were all over him, stinging him. My dad grabbed him up and put him in the water and was picking off the bees. I was screaming so loudly my mom came running out, wanting to know what happened. My dad brought the lifeless pup and laid him on the porch. He said the bees were too much for him. He was still too small. I just cried and cried.

He said, "We will get another one. He had never really showed any interest in me before, so I was just thinking I will never have another one. I loved this puppy, and my heart was broken.

As time went on that summer, my friend Nancy had her own playhouse, and it was filled with toys and candy. I thought she was the luckiest girl in the world. She didn't live with her mom and dad; she lived with her grandparents. We played every chance we got, and sometimes her grandparents would take me into town to get stuff with them.

She was the only friend my mom would allow me to play with, and she lived down the big road but still could walk there. One day, when I was walking down to play with her, an old car pulled up beside me, and this old man said, "Where you going, girlie?"

I said, "To my friend's house."

He said, "Get in, and I will give you a ride there." The thought of my early year experience with my niece came back to me, and I could feel her tightening her hand in mine and the words she said to save us, I said I can see my friends grandpa standing right down there waiting on me and he can see you to and I ran as fast as I could my mom did not allow me to walk there again by myself.

One afternoon, my dad said to me to go to the store and get him some chewing tobacco. The store was up the big road and was quite a walk to get there only one house to pass, and they had a huge Colley dog that would bite and always laid by the road. I simply couldn't believe that he would ask a ten-year-old little girl to do this, but he did I tried to tell him. I was afraid of that dog and it was too far for me to go.

I had never gone there by myself, and he said, "Yes, you can just go straight up there and back."

I fought back tears because I was actually afraid of him more, so he gave me some money, told me what kind to get, and off I went. I just knew that dog would bite me, and I really didn't know what to do but believe someone would watch out for me. I couldn't believe that my mom would allow this. Why would she not stop him from sending me out on that big road?

I finally made it to the house with the dog. I did not see any sign of him. His name was Buzz, so I walked so fast straight ahead, and I was so happy. I made it and then approached the store and went in. The lady there was beautiful. I thought she dressed so nice, and her hair and makeup was perfect.

She said, "Well, hello, young lady, who is with you?"

I said, "No one. My dad sent me here to get his chewing tobacco."

She looked shocked and said, "Are you telling me that he sent you up here by yourself, and you walked on this road alone?"

"Yes, ma'am."

I could tell she did not like this at all, and she did say when she saw my dad, she would have a word with him, so I got the tobacco, and she said her husband could take me home, but I said, "No, that's okay. I will be fine," because I was also afraid of old men.

Her husband was much older than her it seemed. As I made it back down the road to my house, the dog was not out, and I was thinking this was really a miracle. I made it back to the porch, and my dad was sitting there like he was waiting on his chewing tobacco, and I gave it to him his change. Then he asked, "Did you get yourself anything?"

I said, "No, you did not say I could," and went on in the house. No more was ever said about that trip.

my Dad with one of his cats

A couple weeks later, he yelled for me to come out on the porch, so I did, and he had two cats.

He said, "I got you these cats."

I told him I did not like cats. I was afraid of them.

He said, "Well, you can name them."

I told him I really didn't want to name them because I wouldn't play with them, so he named both cats Jutertom and Spundolux, and they hung around him all the time. I stayed clear of both of them.

School started, and the fifth grade was here. I was growing up, going to the store by myself over the summer, and felt grown-up.

Not much happening in fifth grade. Studies were much harder, and I had a hard time keeping up as I did not have school supplies that I needed but tried to make do with what someone would give me. Matt and Zach were still both in high school but seemed to be getting in trouble with the local boys. One evening, they came home, and my dad had a big long switch, and he whipped both of them very hard. I was screaming to him not to hurt them; they had not done anything. Why was he doing this? Why was he being so mean to them? It was all I could think, and I was pulling on my mom to please stop him right now. He was whipping them too hard. She told him then that was enough, and they would learn their lesson. After that, I heard the older ones talking that they had been drinking, and that's why he had to whip them.

All I know after that, Zach quit his senior year of school and went to live with another brother who lived away. I was so sad. All that was left was me and Matt. How would we make it without him looking after us? It was a sad time. I turned eleven, and as usual, no one seemed to care or notice I was getting older but me. No cake, no birthday present, and of course, I never was used to getting anything, but I thought now that my dad was home, living with us, he might remember my birthday and give me a present. The day came and went and nothing. I understood I was the tenth child, and my parents had grandkids when I was born, but I thought, *What did that have to do with me?* I was glad I was here. There must be some purpose for my life, or I wouldn't be here, so I told myself.

A couple more months went by, and as I was going out the door for school, my dad said, "Come here, Latte."

That's what he called me, and I turned around and walked to his chair, and he pulled out a little change purse that snapped together in the middle, and he opened it and said, "I might find you a little something in here."

He never gave me any money ever, and I got a little excited, so he pulled out a quarter and then a nickel and placed it in my hand and said, "Now share this if you want to with Jenny and Noah."

They were my niece and nephew whom I loved and played with so much. Usually, he would push his false teeth out at me and scare me, but he didn't that day. As we went to get on this bus, walking to the bus stop, I shared my good news with Jenny and Noah. We were all so excited we would get a dime apiece. This was awesome. We three all felt rich. What started as a great day ended in sorrow. How could we have known what happened? How did this happen and why?

We got home from school with the news my dad had a heart attack, and all were at the hospital. It didn't look like he would make it through. I didn't know what I felt. The ones who were there were crying and sobbing, and he was not even dead yet. How did they know he would not make it through? Then around 7:00 p.m., everyone came through the door in tears and said he had died. That was all. Everyone would sit around and drink coffee and smoke cigarettes and talk and cry, and the grandkids who were there with me were about four or five, and they would tell us to go play. I didn't know what to do or how to feel. I wasn't sure about how this was going to affect my mom.

my Dad

The next day, a coffin was in our house with my dad in it. It stayed there for two nights so many people came in and out of the house. The yard was filled with people. They were everywhere, and I was told to go play with the kids, so I did. I had just turned eleven, my niece was thirteen and a half, and another was six. My nephews were from three to ten years old. They were several grandkids there, and none of us knew what to do. It was like I was the grandkid, and I guess I was.

The funeral came, and they moved my dad over the old school that was now a church, and there they had his funeral. My niece had to babysit because she was the oldest, and that left me by myself because the other kids did not get to come. I sat alone, and they sang "In the Sweet Bye and Bye" and "We Will Meet at the River." Looking around, I felt I was out of place. Maybe I should be with the grandkids. As the service was over, everyone started to walk up to the coffin. I wanted to say goodbye, but nobody came to take me up or even look my way. I really was scared and didn't know what I should do, so I was sitting there now all alone. No one was left, so I slipped out the side door and ran home.

No one ever mentioned me, not once after the service. I heard my sisters and brothers saying that Jenny should have been there, and this would be very hard for her because my dad loved her so much. I didn't know he loved anyone. I never saw it or was shown in any way and didn't understand why they were talking about it. It was a sad time for me to see my mom cry, and there was nothing I could do. I didn't feel maybe the way I should have about my family and the passing of my dad at that time because no one bothered to ask me to go with them to say goodbye. But later in life, I wished I had gone up by myself and said goodbye to my dad.

I had a dream, and he came in the dream. He was at the top of a hill, waving goodbye to me, and I waved back at him, and he smiled down on me so that helped, and I didn't think much of it anymore. Christmas came and went. My dad had been gone for a couple of weeks now. It was calm around the house. No one had much to say, and I didn't know what to say, so I just kept to myself. We did not have Christmas presents, but we never did unless someone came by to give us something, and I never thought much about it. This was a sad time for my family.

Our family dog, Rex, came in the back door where the kitchen was one evening, and he just looked around, didn't do anything, and my mom was trying to get him out as she did not like dogs in the house. He was just standing there in the kitchen for a moment, and he turned around walked out, and we never saw him again. This was very odd because he was my dad's dog, following him up and down the road and always by his side. I felt he knew something had happened to my dad. Folks on the hollow looked for him, but he was never found.

Matt and I were all that my mom had at home. I had always slept with my mom, and since my dad had come home, my brother slept with him every night. I think my dad's passing affected Matt much more than me because he was starting to become a problem for my mom, staying out late drinking. This was a big worry for her. Zach had left him, and now my dad had passed, leaving him, and he changed more and more each day. I had to take on doing more chores around the house. He would not help do anything, and my mom couldn't do it all. There was just so much to do. I would have to carry the coal onto our porch in a bucket so we would stay warm during the winter. I would have to make several trips across the road from our house because it was very heavy. Matt would not help. If he was there, he would just tell me I had to do it.

coal we used in stove for winter

He became verbally mean, and I was really getting to be afraid of him. I couldn't understand what happened to my good brother and what was going on. My mom did everything she could for my brother as he was treated much differently than me. She would serve him first at breakfast and dinner. I did not mind because I figured my mom knew best, and I was used to seeing the males get served first, as through the years, the men ate first and the kids last. I felt she was getting a little afraid of him. He would hang out at my older sister Patty's house, and they would drink together, and my mom would have to go up to her house and break up fights between them and make sure her babies were okay. My mom would make me stay at the neighbor's house, and I, of course, would worry about her.

My neighbor would say, "It's a shame that Matt and Patty are worrying your mom so much."

I would not say anything. I felt sorry for how my mom had to live. In a short while, she would come by and take me home. I could see she was very worried. Matt would get very mean with her, and I could see the hurt and fear in her face. We would go home, and then early hours in the morning before the day came, he would come in and demand her to get up and make him something to eat.

Spring came and went quickly. My brother had gotten worse. School was out. My mom and I would go visit my sister Ally, and I would play with her kids. There was little age difference between her daughter's and me, and we always played together, and we loved each other very much and always had a good time playing together. They had a big claw-foot bathtub, and I felt like a princess when I got to take a bath in it as I had to bathe in a washtub, and my mom would heat water on the stove, so this was a real treat for me, and I loved it.

Sixth and seventh grades passed quickly. I had a really hard time going to school with my brother. I was still sleeping with my mom. I never had my own room, and it was hard to sleep with my brother yelling all the time through the night. He would insist on my mom getting up and fixing him something to eat, and he would finally go to bed around three or four in the morning, and I would have to be so quiet and not make a sound.

I was not getting the sleep I needed, and I was suffering from fear with Matt. I did not have what I needed for school, no supplies, paper, or pencils. This was making it hard for me to focus on classes. There was always a struggle with something, and it was very hard, but I did what I had to during this time and did not complain about anything to just help my mom. Bullying was still an issue at school; however, the kids knew I had lost my dad in fifth grade and was not quite so bad I could deal with it. I had much bigger problems at home.

my school from 3rd grade through 8th

Eighth grade was probably my best year, but still a few very dark times, I started my menstrual cycle, and I didn't know what was happening. I thought I was dying and didn't know who to tell and what to do. Jenny and I were playing. We had an outside bathroom, which was called a toilet, and there were big cracks through the door. My niece saw all the blood I guess and went screaming to my mom, so I started to cry. I came into the house through the kitchen, and all who was there just stared at me and was laughing. We had a big cold stove in the living room, and even in summer, my mom used it to cook beans on, and we would roast potatoes around the bottom where it was so hot. That's what the family was doing at that time, roasting some potatoes. Looking at me and laughing, I thought they didn't care that I was dying, and then my mom said, "Come on back here with me." She pulled out a big white cloth, folded it, and told me to put this on to catch the blood. Nothing else was ever said, not my niece or any of my four older sisters explained to me what was happening. The bleeding finally stopped and went back to normal.

A month later in the classroom, I got up from my seat, and it was covered in blood. All the kids looked and started laughing. I had no clue on what to do; I did not have a white cloth with me.

I did have a good teacher. Actually I had two great teachers in the eighth grade. They were husband and wife. So the wife came to me and asked if this was my first time. I said no, embarrassed to talk about it, and she explained everything to me and got me the sanitary napkins that I needed, and that was one less worry I had. I knew I was not dying now. To think I had never seen a sanitary napkin and didn't know what they were was even more embarrassing. This was such a relief, and this should not have been up to a teacher to explain this to me, not a friend would even tell me, and later I found out all my friends had started their cycles.

my 8th grade picture

There was an opportunity came up that the top five students in the eighth grade got picked to go to Washington, DC, and, yes, I was one of those students who sure didn't know how I could make the list with not getting enough sleep that I needed and also having to sleep in my clothes for school and to not make any noise to wake my brother. He had quit school by now and was just causing more and more worry on my mom. I had to leave for school without washing my face and brushing my teeth. This later caused me to have gum disease that I have dealt with through the years.

My mom said I could not go on the trip. We had no money, and my niece Jenny did not want me to go. She was a sophomore in high school, and they did not get to go, so she told my mom also not to allow me to go. I think she was just worried about me going with other school students whom I didn't know. My teacher and another parent came to my mom, told her it would be a great trip for me, and they would fund my trip, and this would not cost her any money. So with that offer, she allowed me to go. It was a wonderful trip with so many other kids from different schools. She had packed me a brown bag lunch to take with me, had ham sandwich, and some chips and candy. When the bus stopped at a McDonalds, all the kids were very excited and got off and ordered their lunch. I had never been to or seen a McDonalds. The food smelled so good and looked very good, but I sat and ate my ham sandwich my mom fixed for me, and I was fine. I had a great time, and I had always had in my heart there were more out there than I was seeing in the hollow I now lived in and just keeping the faith through my first twelve years.

I had been to church and Bible school just a few times, and that was enough to show me there was more than I could see, and I knew I had an angel watching over me. I just knew it, or how else could I survive? I declare this as an act of grace from God and was thankful and grateful.

I had finally reached the age of thirteen, finishing out the eighth grade and passing into high school. There had been no little boyfriends since Tuffy in the first grade. I had never met or had another friend like him. Summer came, and my mom and I went to go visit my oldest sister Jean. I love to play Jenny and Noah with during the visit.

creek where Noah Jenny and me made our own swimming pool

Jenny was fifteen now, and she had friends who lived nearby her house and had a huge pond on their property. They invited us over, and we had pizza and chips like a little party. It was a lot of fun for us, and, yes, that pond became a swimming pool, and Jenny being the protective person, she strapped me into a life jacket along with her little brother as neither he nor I could swim and tighten it until we could hardly breathe and off we went and got in the water. I was afraid, but I wanted to be a grown-up like her, and so in the pond, we went, and just about the time, we got in and was having fun splashing around the water. My sister Jean and my mom had gone by in a car and saw us in that pond and came and got us, and Jenny got a bad whipping for getting in that pond, but Noah and I didn't. I guess my mom was just happy I didn't drown, and Jenny took the whipping for both her and Noah. I didn't like that Jenny got a whipping like that because she was very cautious and kept us safe. I was mad at Jean for a long time after that. We sure did have fun for a little while that day. Later when all the talk was over about the pond and dangers, we would all go biking and ride for hours, enjoying our time together. They were more like my brother and sister than my family was, and I felt a real closeness to them.

Summer passed, and I started my freshman year of high school. I had high hopes that my life would be good, and I would fit in with the kids. I was a shy timid girl and had a hard time making friends, but I had not been a bother to my mom. She had enough problems with my brother Matt.

The first day of school came. I was excited to be in high school. It was not bad. I think everyone was excited and a little nervous, even the older kids I saw in the hall. I made it through the day, and riding the big high school bus was scary and exciting. All the older kids that were tenth, eleventh, and twelfth grade on the bus, and they would make jokes and wisecracks about freshman students, but I just sat there with the others.

As time went on, I still sometimes had to sleep in my clothes but was able to wash my face or brush my teeth before going off to high school by tiptoeing around and had to leave with no breakfast, maybe a piece of cake or bread, due to noise it would make in the kitchen, waking up Matt. I wondered if other kids would notice my wrinkled clothes, and I was sure they did as I got stares at school from so many kids. Life was hard with my brother Matt. He was not getting better; he was much worse. My older brothers tried to help him, but he still was rebelling against something. I wasn't sure I could make it through high school doing my work that I had living like this.

my Mom

40

A few months went by, and my mom told me we may have to move out of state in with my sister Lou because she could not handle Matt anymore.

I asked, "What about school?"

She said, "There is a school where I can go to."

I didn't say anything because I knew things could not go on as they had, and it couldn't get any worse moving and going to another school, and besides the drinking, my brother was also doing some drugs, making it more dangerous to be around with my mom and me.

In January, on a cold winter morning, we moved in with my sister. Second semester was beginning, and I was taken to enroll in my new school. It was a huge school. It was like a college. It was very scary; I thought I will never find my way here. It was a very cold, and the snow would fall deep there in the winter, and my first day at my new school would be here soon. No one had advised me on which bus or even if there was a bus to take to the school, so that was on my mind, but I figured someone would show me or take me. To get me ready for my first day of school, Lou asked me to have a new haircut. She was a beautician, and she took me to her shop where she worked to fix my hair. I had no idea what was about to happen to me.

me at age 14

I liked my hair. It was very black and hanged between my neck and shoulders, but that all changed in about thirty minutes. My sister sat me in her chair and put a plastic cap on my head and took a big pick that look like a darning needle and started pulling strings of hair out pieces at a time. I was crying, saying, "What are you doing this for?"

She said, "Oh, you will love it when I am done."

I didn't; I hated it. She cut off all my hair as short as it was cut when I was in fifth grade. I was so sad thinking why had this happened, but I knew she was trying to help me get off to a new and good start at my new school. I know Lou meant well, and maybe she wanted me to look more like her since I was her little sister, but I didn't. She had always been beautiful, but I was okay with myself and didn't need to look different or like anyone else.

My hair was almost white blond; I hated it. I looked so different. My mom loved it, and I think that's because Lou was a total blond. I went back to her house and found a place and cried and felt so awful about myself. Now the kids would make fun of me for sure. I was grateful we had a nice place to come and stay and was happy for my mom. So I acted as I loved it to her because I didn't want to hurt her feelings. She was just trying to help me. I felt so lost and missed what few friends I had at home.

Somehow, I knew something would need to happen by grace to help me through this.

The first day of school arrived, and my sister took me and dropped me off and talked about a little lost sheep, but that was me. I had no idea where I was going. Never had I been in a place so big. As I was walking down the long halls, looking for my class, I could see less and less students in the hall. All was going into their classes. I heard a loud bell ring, and I was alone in the hall. Finally, by the grace of God, I came upon my classroom door, and I slowly opened it and went in. Everyone was staring hard at me, and the teacher said, "You are late."

I just looked at him and shyly said, "Sorry I couldn't find the room," and everyone laughed. I took an empty seat and felt like a fish out of water. No one tried to be friendly and say, "Hi, where you from?" or anything, so when the class was over, I was so nervous about how I was going to find the next class, and again I was late I ended up being late for every class that day, but I knew if I could remember, I would never be late again.

The first day wasn't too bad but not good either. I survived, and that's what counted.

My sister picked me up that first day but told me I had to ride the bus from now on because she worked and had to be home with her toddler. She was a little beauty in nursery school. So here went another huge worry about what I was to do and how could I handle this.

I had just turned fourteen and was growing up quickly. I went from falling off a porch with this being one of the sisters who let it happen to now live in her home and with her family, trying to go to a strange and huge school. I was thankful to have a safe place to live and to sleep. My fears went from thinking Matt would hurt my mom and me to how I was going to get to and from the big school.

The next morning, I walked downtown. It was very cold to find the place to get on the bus. I walked to a bus stop, and I never saw any school bus come by, so I knew the way to walk to school, so off I went thinking back to third grade and getting a whipping. I had never forgotten, but this was high school now, and surely I would not get into any trouble. It seemed like hours, but I finally made it. I had walked to school all by myself. It was by grace I found the school and my way. I, again, was late getting to my classes as it was still difficult to find my way through the hallways to the different classrooms. Finally, the second day came to an end, and I was worried about what bus I needed to be on. I walked out with other kids who were riding the bus, thinking I was getting on the right one, and as I watched all the other kids getting off at their homes, no place looked familiar to me, not that it would, but I knew where I now lived. As the last kid got off the bus, the driver turned around and looked very stern, saying, "Where do you live? This is the last stop of the day."

I told him where I lived, and he said, "You got on the wrong bus. I cannot take you there. The only thing I can do is take you and drop you off in town."

I was thrilled because I knew I could walk home from there. I said thank you. I was so shy to speak up and had no one to speak for me, so I never rode the bus again, and I walked every day, and that was very hard as it was so cold and snowed every week that winter. Until one day, a cute young boy at school named Harry asked me my name and where I was from. I told him, and he asked if he could pick me up and take me to school. I was thrilled not to have to walk, so I said yes, and then it all started.

I was trying hard at this school because I like the living arrangements we had with my sister Lou and wondered why my mom and I had to live with such difficulty since my father died and why we did not have the things we needed, so I was determined to do my best to make things better.

My mom started working for a couple that had three kids and lived with them as their nanny and housekeeper. This was hard for me, but I understood. My sister Lou only had two bedrooms, and the one we had was small and was most likely her little two-year-old baby girl, and we had come and moved in and took it over. Her little girl slept in a small toddler bed beside their big bed, and it seemed to work out. Her little girl went to nursery daycare while she worked.

Another day of school came, and Harry showed up, and off I went. I was so shy I never said a word all the way to school. He was very tall and good-looking, and I looked older than my age. Thanks to my sister with the short-bleached hair.

He walked me to my class and said, "I will see you later." I said okay. Later that day, as I was going down the hall for lunch, we had to go around a corner and down the steep stairs to the lunchroom. As I had topped the stairs, Harry yelled out, "Wait up! I will walk with you."

I got nervous and fell straight down those stairs all the way to the bottom. It was the most embarrassing moment I had so far as a teenager. This was so bad. I thought I was hurt bad. Everyone started to gather around me to see if I was okay. It was a bad fall; however, nothing was broken, except my pride was crushed. I kept to myself after that day and never talked to anyone. Everyone seems to be staring at me all the time, and I didn't know how to react. What was wrong with me? Why was I this way? I never told Lou or my mom I fell. I knew they would have a good laugh, and it wasn't funny. I would just be more humiliated and hurt.

I see Harry the next day at school, and he came and said, "I tried to get to you when you fell, and you were gone. I'm so sorry I feel awful. Are you okay?"

I said, "Sure, I am fine," knowing my bruises were covered up, and I refused to show my pain. He walked me to class and asked me to go out with him, and I said okay. I did tell Lou and my mom that he asked me out, and I said yes, knowing I was only fourteen. My mom said that it was okay for me to go.

My sister said she was going to fix me up with her landlord's grandson. She said he would be a good guy for me. I had never had a boyfriend, just a guy being nice, picking me up one day for school, and I embarrassed myself by tumbling down a flight of stairs. But I had agreed to go out with him on a date, and he could pick me up after school. Lou did fix me up with the landlord's grandson, and the day came, and my brother-in-law Steve helped me get ready for my blind date. My sister fixed my short blond hair and all teased it all up. I wore a short mini dress and a fur coat. It was in beginning March, the doorbell rang, and this guy came in, wore glasses, and had big hair my mom had approved of earlier but was not there as she had to work.

He looked and me and said wow.

I thought, *How old are you? And why are these people allowing me to go out on a date by myself? I am only fourteen, not even fourteen and a half.*

But they did and said, "Have fun."

We got in this brand-new car. It was a GTO, and off we went. He took me to a very nice fancy restaurant called the Lamppost, and everyone turned around and was staring at us. He was holding his hand on my back, and I thought we must look good or not as I was used to people staring at me a lot. As we were seated, he looked like he was just beaming with joy. I didn't know why, and when he ordered something to drink and I had no clue on what to order, so I said I would have the same.

He was shaking his head no, but the lady said okay. It was a mixed alcoholic drink he ordered, and I guess I passed the age limit from how I was dressed and looked. He said, "Sorry, but you can't have that," and ordered me a Coke. My food that night was spaghetti, and he showed me how to eat it. I had not seen spaghetti being eaten using a spoon before. He, I think, he was in awe of me and treated me like I was a princess. He was very polite and told me I was a very young lady and took me home. He did not try to kiss me or anything; he would open the door for me, take my hand, and help me out. That was it. I had never been kissed or thought about it. That still kind of stuff was in the gross stage for me. But for the first time, I felt someone just may truly care about me.

I did not know how to act or how someone should be treated, but this young man sure set high standards for me to continue in my life after him. I knew that I would never accept anything less than this now.

A few days went by, and I did not hear from him, so Harry from school stopped by to pick me up for school and asked if he could pick me up the next day, and I said okay, and he promised not to yell out for my attention near the stairs ever again, and we laughed. He was a nice guy, and I liked him.

Another day came and went, and Harry was waiting on me, and about the time I was getting in his car, the big new GTO pulled in right behind him. It had been over a week since my date with Lynn, and I had not spoken to him and didn't know why he was there. I thought maybe he was there to see my sister Lou, so we pulled out.

Harry said, "Who was that guy? He got awfully close to my car there. How do you know him?"

I said, "My sister knows his family, and she fixed me up with him, and we went on a date."

He kind of looked funny and said, "Your mom allows you to go out on an actual date at fourteen?"

"I guess."

We got to school. He walked me to my locker and said he would see me later.

That evening, the guy Lynn with the GTO came by my sister's house and told me he would be picking me up from now on and taking me to school and asked who that guy was whom I went with this morning. I told him he was my friend from school, and he said I would not need him anymore. Keep in mind, I was just barely over fourteen, and I had not had much attention to speak of in my few years on earth, so I was kind of liking this, and I said okay. The next morning, he was there to pick me up on time and walked right into school with me to my locker.

I asked him, "Why you are coming in with me?"

He said, "Just making sure you are okay." I guess looking back, it was to let all the guys know I was taken. I had no idea what was going on but was liking the attention, and mainly the ride to school was most important to me.

Lynn said, "I will walk you to your first class."

There was Harry in the hallway with some other guys, and they appeared to have stunned looks on their faces. Later that day, Harry said, "Who was that older guy with you?"

I said, "He is a friend whom I went out to eat with."

"Was that the guy in your driveway?" and I said

"Yes, I told you about it yesterday."

"I just can't believe that your mom would be okay with this."

"Well, she is, and she really likes him, and he wants to pick me up and bring me to school every day."

He looked hurt, and I really didn't know at that moment how I felt because I liked both guys, but Lynn had kind of taken charge of my situation.

He said, "How old is that guy?"

"I don't know."

"He is much too old for you."

I asked my sister how old he was that evening when I got home from school, and she said twenty-one. I, of course, did not know he could go to jail for hanging around me and why, if it was so bad, would my mom agree and want me to go out with him.

Thereafter, every day, he would pick me up early and take me to breakfast and pick me up every evening and bring me home. He treated me like a little princess, was never disrespectful, and would brush a kiss lightly across my lips. I had never been kissed. I was spending a lot of time with this man. When we would go into restaurants, people would just stare hard at us, and I did not know why. Maybe it was because he had on work clothes in the mornings when we stop to eat breakfast as he worked at night on a job. He took good care of me the remaining year of school and got very serious. He said I was a wonderment of the world. He was so good to me. Never once tried to do anything to me that would hurt me. He was a complete gentleman in every way.

God had to put this man here for me to finally get a good start in life, knowing how a man should treat a young girl or woman or in my case a boy to treat a girl. I had not witnessed that so far in my life. I had never seen anything that had impressed me in my own family. He would take me to his house, and it was so beautiful, and he would cook for me and make things I had never had. If I were rich, I wanted to live like this. I really did feel like a princess.

Schooltime was almost over, and I knew my mom and I would be going home for the summer to give my sister a break, and he began to tell me how he would miss me and how much he loved me and wanted to make a home for me with him.

I said, "But I am only fourteen. How can that happen?"

He said, "Leave it to me, and I will always take good care of you."

My life had been up and down throughout, and I really liked him so much and the idea someone would take care of me. He said he would make sure I got through school and college and be there always for me. This man truly loved me, and for me, that was something I had never felt I had gotten from anyone before. I had grown up fast and didn't understand about feelings like this, and there was no one I could talk to about it.

He was simply an awesome man. Before we left to come home for the summer, he asked my mom when I turned fifteen, if he could marry me, and she said yes, and she would sign for me, so it was settled. I would be married when I turned fifteen that year. I would be in tenth grade. I mean, who does this or thinks like this for their fifteen-year-old daughter?

That summer, while we were home, we rode a Greyhound bus to visit my aunt Ethel out of town to the big city. Lynn's mom lived close to my aunt, and he set it up for me to come to stay with his mom and him for the week we were there. My aunt went crazy when she found out how old he was; she and my mom got into a huge argument. I felt bad because I didn't like to see anyone be upset, especially my mom, and when he showed up with his mom, my aunt told them I was not going anywhere with a twenty-one-year-old man that she could have him locked up.

my aunt Ethel

I did not understand why my aunt was so upset. This was a good and decent man who had treated me like a princess since I had met him. That's exactly how she had treated me when I would visit her as a child. My mom apologized to his mom and him and told my aunt that she was my mom, and I could go. I left without my aunt's approval, and I didn't think his mom was happy either, but when we got to her home, she had me set up to sleep in his sisters' room, and we had fun all week. I had never seen anyone cook out on a grill before it was so cool, and he was very good at it. They were very rich. He had taken a vacation from his job to come down that week to see me. I was very happy, having a great time. We would ride bikes through the neighborhood and go to the movies with his brother and his girlfriend. I don't think they approved of the relationship as they never had much to say when we were out. I was shy and didn't speak often.

We went shopping, and he bought us matching Mickey Mouse shirts that were just so cool to me. He knew how to treat a girl, but I guess the reason was he was much older and was a true gentleman and being a military Marine maybe helped also. One night, I broke a beautiful lamp on the nightstand in his sister's room. I was so upset and embarrassed I cried to him and said I was sorry.

He just held me tight in his arms and said, "Don't worry. I will take care of it." He told his mom he broke the lamp and would replace it, and I could tell she did not believe him. She asked him how he broke it, and when was he in my room, he said, "I went in to just say goodnight," and went on to say, "I will replace it."

Later that week, she came to me and said, "Who really broke that lamp? Be truthful to me."

I had never been so scared in my life, but I knew I had to tell her the truth. I was staying in her home and owed her the respect to do the right thing. I told her what happened, and I was sorry.

She said, "You shouldn't have let my son take the blame."

"I didn't tell him to say it wasn't me."

I didn't think she cared too much for me, and I could not blame her as I was a fifteen-year-old girl who put her son in danger with an underage girl at his age.

The week ended, and it was time to go back to my aunt's for the last night before going back home. He was so sad. The week was ending. He continually told me how much I meant to him and how much he loved me and wanted me to be with him forever and couldn't wait for a few more months to pass. I was excited, thinking this was going to be my good life. When we arrived at my aunt's home, she apologized to him and said no one would ever be good enough for me, and he better know it. It was a weird apology as she really let him have it again in a different sort of way. He accepted her apology and was very polite. After he left, she took me outside, set me down, and wanted to know everything my mom had never asked me one time, or no one else had ever ask. She started out saying I am going to ask you some questions and be truthful with me: These are the questions she asked, how he treated me, where he touched me, where he took me, how did I know him, on and on, and I would answer and tell her the complete truth.

She said, "Honey, you know he is much too old for you. A twenty-one-year-old man has no business with a child."

I told her how he had helped me get through my freshman year of high school. I really didn't think I would have made it if not for him. My mom was staying away, working. My sister had a two-year-old; it was too much. No one had time for me.

She looked at me and put her arm around me and said, "I know it's been hard for you and your mom, and I wish I could make it right for you, but everything will work for the good through time for you, just don't rush into anything that will affect the rest of your life."

She was still mad at my mom, but she wouldn't back down. She really didn't want me to marry this man.

We went home, and I had not had a chance to tell my friends I was getting married. It became the laughingstock among all of them. They said that was the craziest thing they ever heard.

They said, "We will not let this happen to you. We want you to stay home and have fun with us."

The most fun I had was being with him and when I was little being with Noah playing. My oldest brother Carl and his wife and three kids had come down to stay the usual two weeks for the summer, and yes, he thought my mom had lost her mind to allow something like this to even be thought of. His wife was a very classy and smart lady. She took me aside and asked if he had touched me in private places, and blushing red, I said, "Oh no, he would never do that. He only lightly brushes kisses over my lips and face. He treats me like a princess."

She said, "You know if he did, he could go to jail for the rest of his life."

"He is not like that."

So she went on to say if she spoke with my brother and he said it was okay, I could come live with them. She was scaring me a little with all this talk, and I was beginning to wonder if or why this was wrong. She came back the next day to me and said it was okay with Carl for me to come to live with them, and they would send me to school and take care of me. I told my mom, and she was so angry. I had not seen that side of her in that way as she was angry with my aunt Ethel, but nothing like this. She told my sister-in-law to tend to her own business that I would not be going home with them that I had someone who was good to me and would take care of me and to keep out of it.

I was torn because I really took everything she said and thought about my life. I was just a kid who had to grow up much too fast.

When they left early going back home, she gave me a tight hug and said, "Remember you don't have to do this. You have us to come to."

I said, "My mom won't allow me to."

"Carl will take care of your mom."

They left, and my mom was not sorry to see them go.

She said, "They should tend to their own business."

Then a couple days went by, and one of my friends wanted me to go out with her and her boyfriend on a double date with one of his friends, and I said, "I can't do that. I am getting married in a few months."

She laughed and said, "Well, that's a few months away. This won't hurt, and I can't go unless you go, so we can double."

I asked my mom, and she said no. I begged and told her I was just helping my friend out, and she finally agreed, so these guys picked us up. I did not know them but was introduced, and the guy for me seemed to really like what he saw in me and was kind of cute. I was going into tenth grade; my friend's boyfriend was going into twelfth grade. We had a fun time, went to a movie, and ate, and when the guy I was with pulled me in for a kiss, I didn't resist and kind of liked it but felt strong guilt come over me. What kind of person was I cheating on my boyfriend? So I pulled away quickly and told him I already had a boyfriend. I had been dating for several months. We talked, and the night ended. He said he would really like to see me again, and I said, "We will see." Later again, some friends went out, and more guys were coming around who liked me, but I wouldn't date any of them.

The summer was coming to an end, and I talked to my boyfriend every day. He would call me to want to know how I was doing, and he was getting me lots of presents and couldn't wait to see me. I felt guilty; I really did.

My sister and her four kids came down to stay a week with my mom. The house was crazy, and we were busy. It was so hot; we had no air-conditioner. It was awful. She had two kids in diapers, and the house smelled of soiled diapers.

One unexpected day, he called and said, "Guess what? I got off a few days, and I bought your engagement ring. I can't wait any longer. I want to come down to your home and see you and bring it and put it on your finger, so everyone will know you are mine."

I was so surprised and speechless. I could not say anything, and after a pause, he said, "Are you okay? What's wrong?"

I started to cry and told him everything that was going on and what my sister-in-law had said to me along with my aunt and friends, and he said, "What does this mean? What are you trying to tell me?"

I said, "I don't know. I guess I don't think I am ready to get married. I am just a kid."

"No, you are not a kid. Please don't do this to us. You are an amazing young lady whom I love more than anything in the world and only want the best for you in life. I will take care of you."

He started to cry and said, "Please let me come get you and make you mine forever." He couldn't believe I had come back home, and they talked me out of my life. I told him we could talk again and to give me a few days.

I told my mom I wanted to go to school at home this year, and she was very upset and asked me what had happened.

I thought, *Well, I know I broke my heart, as well as his. I felt worthless. Why was this happening to me? Why was I a disappointment? What should I do?*

This was a sad time. I could see the look in my mom's eyes. She didn't say much, but I could tell she was deeply hurt. Looking back, I think she saw a way out for her, as well as me. She only wanted a good life for me, and she sure deserved one herself. If only I had been a little older, maybe it would have worked out. I had no experience in life, just growing up so fast. I did not know what to do, and it was very hard. I would find myself alone crying all the time, wondering if I had made the right decision, and how could I hurt someone who had been so good to me and probably saved my life for months.

My tenth year of school was almost here. I was still fourteen but soon would be fifteen, the time I was supposed to be married. My mom was very quiet lately, not talking about much of anything, and I tried to put on a happy face and go visit my friends, but it was lonely. I guess I was missing my boyfriend, and then school started, and everything started to work out. My brother Matt had left again, and it was just my mom and me, and we seemed to be doing okay. She was afraid sometimes at night, and during the middle of the night, we would have to walk through the long path and go over to my older brother Frank's house and then walk back at daybreak for me to get ready for school. This happened several nights.

A few months went by, and again Matt showed up, and my mom said. "You will have to go back to the school you went to last year."

I said, "Oh no, I don't want to go back now I was doing good in school," and I was trying hard to make my way. But I did not have a choice, and neither did she. We had to leave because she and I couldn't see any peace at our home. I think I now realize what marriage meant for my mom, having someone to take care of me and a place for her because he always said my mother would have a place in our home, and he had told her that.

I thought, *Did I make the right decision? Should I have done what my mom wanted me to do?* Somehow deep down, I had faith that everything would be okay.

Same time in January, I started school again. I had a few hard classes in geometry and a hard science class, and I knew it would be more difficult in this school, so I tried to prepare myself. I also had health and PE class. All we do was go out at my school and do jumping jacks and stretches. We did not have any equipment to work on, but we did have a great teacher and studied good health. Some of the kids remembered me from the year before, and I did not have anyone to pick me up, so I had to walk, and it was very cold. I felt alone and lonely, missing that special someone. I had a very hard time adjusting to these tenth-grade classes. The teaching was different, and half a year had gone by again, and I was struggling not only in geometry but also health and PE class. They had trampoline bars and things I had never seen before, and we had to have PE outfits, and because I would not shower in front of the class after it was over, I got a D minus. I was very shy and just would not take off my clothes and get the shower. My teacher was very upsetting; she did not like me. There was nothing I could do, and she did not show any mercy, kind of a reminder of my first-grade teacher. No one wanted to be made fun of, and the other kids made fun and laughed at me for not doing what she said. They would say things like, "Why not take a shower?" "Do you have one at home?" "Is there something wrong with you?" It was just stuff to bully me, and God knows I had been used too much of that during my years, so I knew I could handle this. I would show them. I had to become a stronger person.

It was very difficult going into such a dramatic change. Our school was not fortunate enough to have the equipment they had, and I had never seen any of these things and was so far behind all the sophomore class here. They were very good, and I was a mess, but I tried hard. I finally got the trampoline down and was doing pretty good and even the balance bar. I could walk but not flip on it, and the teacher finally told me I would not be allowed to participate in class if I did not shower with the team. So that was it. I did not get to do anything else, and I had really liked it, but no way was I stripping down in front of a bunch of girls and taking a shower. That was the end of my health and PE class.

Then there was the speech class that I had not had and was told to prepare an oral report in front of the class. This was for all students, and I said I could not do it. I was so shy; it was impossible. The teacher said I had no option that would be my grade, or I would get an F in the class, and I knew I was failing health and PE, and I would never get out of school or have an opportunity to graduate if something didn't give for me.

I told my sister, and she said, "You can do it, just get up and do your report, and you will be fine."

I worried far too much about this and went back to the teacher and said, "I just can't do it."

He said, "You should never say *can't* in your vocabulary."

"Is there anything else I can do?"

"Type a ten-page book report or get up and do one paragraph of an oral report."

"I will type the report."

He looked stunned and said, "Are you serious?"

"Yes, sir, I am."

I typed a ten-page report on a manual typewriter, and yes, that was stupid. Looking back and wishing many times I had gotten up there, but knowing the students would laugh and most likely make fun as kids had before, it was not worth it.

I turned in the report, and the class was amazed. They said they had looked forward to my time doing my report. I was a little doubtful of their sincerity, but maybe they were being truthful. But I would never know, and not allowing myself to stand up was a huge mistake in that class and in my life.

I would think about things on my way home in the evenings. It was a really long walk to where I lived with my sister Lou. Why was this going to be my story? What was the reason for this to be happening? And what was the outcome going to be? Somehow, I knew I was going to make it through, just didn't know how and when this part would be over.

Snow was falling, and as I was leaving school one day, I remember there was quite a big snow on the ground, and I thought, *This is going to be a challenge for me today to get home.* No one was there to pick me up, and I did not have friends to get a ride with, so I was on my own, and I was on my way, walking as fast as I could in the snow. All of a sudden, I started getting hit with hard snowballs. When I turned around, a couple of guys were, I guess, having fun throwing at me, so I started walking faster and faster but took some hard hits.

I yelled and said, "Please stop! I have a long way to walk home and will freeze."

They had their fun and let me go, but I was almost in tears by then, feeling helpless and scared as I had many times before. I thought, *Should I call Lynn and tell him I need him back again.* Oh, I was so ashamed of what I did to him and wondered if he would ever forgive me, but I held on and said to myself, "You can do this. You are strong. Keep the faith." That was a hard day, but I made it home safe and sound. My mom was staying with the same lady she had the year before, so I didn't see her much. I felt very lonely much of the time and missed Lynn. But now I had no one to help me, so I was totally on my own at school and getting to and from.

My sister got me a short blond wig to wear to school. She must have not liked my hair growing out dark again, and I wasn't going to allow her to cut it again and bleach it out. That was not going to happen. But I did wear the blond wig, but all the kids in class said they like my real hair better. One day, when I showed up at school, the halls were filled with older students lining the sides. You could hardly walk by. It was very scary. The news was there was a fight with two of the students that had ended with one of the boys getting expelled, and the other did not, so the college had taken time to come to our high school and protest and said it was unfair. They stayed all day, and I was very afraid. I had gone to the office and tried to call my sister to come to get me, and I could not reach her and did not know how to reach my mom.

So the end of the day came, and I tried to rush and get a head start. Walking home, I had to go across a very long bridge on the main highway, and that was a scary part. There was no room to pass anyone on the narrow walkway, and the street was very busy. When I got on the bridge about a quarter of the way, there came a crowd of big guys, sure part of the protestors who seem to be looking for trouble, and I looked behind me and saw a couple coming behind me as well. This was a time I surely thought my life would be over. Then as we got closer, I could tell they were like a gang, and I was in trouble. There was nothing I could do but pray to my Lord to help me. Just then my sister pulled up and said, "Get in quickly," and I did not waste any time as there was nowhere to go, and they had me blocked on both ends. All I could say was "Thank you, Lord."

She had said she heard there were protests and riots going on at my school and decided she should come get me. Believe me, she was just in time to save me. I missed a couple days of school for things to settle down and then back I went and made it through another year. I met a couple of nice students who would give me a ride home but didn't have any boys who seem interested in me. I think they remembered the year before with the older man. Spring came and went. I looked forward to the warm weather, walking to and from school. Lou got us in a swimming class at the YMCA down the street from her home. We went each week and earned a lifeguard certificate. I really enjoyed this time with Lou.

My sister had fun parties with music and dancing at her house. Everyone always appeared to have a good time. I was fifteen but learned a lot and had grown up very quickly. I guess they were just teaching me things they thought I needed to know and starting me at an early age. I appreciated having a place to stay and go to a school that was nice and had a wonderful sister that allowed my Mom and I to live with her. I could take a bath every night and brush my teeth and feel clean. Our house in Kentucky still had no running water or inside bathroom.

My beautiful sister was very good to me and watched after me as much as she could. One of the guys that worked with my brother in law wanted to go out on a date with me and was thought to be a good guy. He picked me up, took me to a very crazy party with drugs and drinking, things that I should have not been exposed to and were too much for me to see. I had not been touched in any disrespectful way from my Lynn, but this guy was very different, nothing like what my brother-in-law had thought. I told him I was going to tell on him and to take me home. They were drinking, and I told him I was only fifteen. He got scared and took me home. He said he thought I was eighteen.

I said, "No, I am not. Please take me home now."

He did, and his name was never mentioned.

I was in yet another very bad situation, but by grace, I got home safe. After that, I did not go out again with anyone. Sometimes I would sit and miss my boyfriend who treated me like a princess and thought no one may not ever treat me like that again. My mom was still working for the lady with three kids and rarely see her. I was still pretty much on my own again, but I was very careful going to and from school. I met another guy who befriended me and would walk with me in the evenings. He was a cool boy, not very good-looking but seem to want to be my friend, so that lasted for a while, and I enjoyed the company. I never knew where he lived and where he went after I got home. After I would get home each evening, I would go through the back alley down to a little store that sold comic books and candy. I loved comic books and would get one about every day my mom would have money to give me from her job, and I used it wisely, only spending what I needed to.

I think back now, and it scares me knowing the place I was walking surely wasn't safe, but I went about every evening and would stay in the store and looked around at all the comic books and just wanted to take all of them home with me. I didn't have any friends who would call me from school or want to come and hang out with me. I would get letters from a couple of friends from back home, and I would write letters back to them. They would want to know everything about school, if I had another boyfriend, etc., I would tell them no, and that I wanted to come back home, but we couldn't. I really thought they missed me just a little.

Summer came, and school was out, and I was excited to be going home, but my mom had to find out where my brother was and how he was doing before we could leave. I would pray he was okay and somewhere living in another state happy and would stay away from my mom and me. It wasn't long before we were on our way home, and I knew my sister would be glad to get her home back, and she would miss me being there because before we would go home in the summer, she would take me and her kids to the beach with her friend, and we would have a lot of fun. The first time I went, I got the worst sunburn, and it took weeks to heal. It was the worst hurt I think I ever had. I guess no one knew what sunscreen was back then.

Zack, mom, and me

Carl and his family came back for their vacation with us. My mom always looked forward to seeing him because that's the only time he came in through the year. They had fought the year before over me getting married at fifteen, so I did not know how this year would go. His youngest child wore cloth diapers, and our house would stink bad because he would wear them and not get changed as he should have often. My sister Ally would usually come down with her kids for a couple of weeks. Also sometimes they would overlap, and all would be there just a few days at the same time. It could get chaotic at our house in the summer. I would not like it unless I could be outside playing with the kids. Usually I had to be washing dishes from all the food my mom cooked for them.

Sometimes, my nephew, Josh, and I would fight over just about anything. We were about the same age and would argue. He seemed to think he was right about everything and knew more than me about things, but I did not think that was true, so I would fight back, and we had done this back and forth since we were ten and eleven. One time in an actual fight, tearing into each other, my mom broke us up and got into an argument with his mom, and they left going home early. Everyone was mad, and I felt awful again, thinking this was my fault. Before this, everything had been fine, and if they had just left us alone, we would have been okay. They didn't come back until the next summer, but we never actually fought again, but we sure had some good arguments. I didn't think Carl liked me very much after that. He would take all the kids to get ice cream and leave me out. Who does that to a kid? He never acted like I was around, never speaking me. He was much different than my other brothers. I was glad that I never went to live with him and his family, even though it was a nice invitation.

He would also give Jenny and Noah a handful of pocket change every time he came to visit and not give me any, and I was right there with them. He wouldn't even tell them to share with me. Never was sure why he did things like that because I was as poor or more so than any of the other kids. They all still had their dads, and I did not. I got my feelings hurt deeply many times during that summer, and I would find myself crying and missing Lynn as he would know what to do and how to take care of me, but I would hold on that somewhere somehow better things and times were coming. They just had to be, and I believed.

Summer was over, and all had left gone home, and it was just my mom and me again. Matt was off somewhere, and we didn't have to worry too much about him showing up again. He was twenty years old now. Mom always would have a worry look on her face and sometimes sad. I still wondered if she would ever forgive me for breaking Lynn's heart and hers as well.

For our food, my mom would call the local grocer and have our food delivered. She would make a list and just get the things we had to have. Sometimes she would get extra like a pizza in a box, and we would make together. It was my favorite thing to eat and fix. We would be okay for a while.

My brother-in-law worked in a big city that used white paint, and he had brought my mom a five-gallon can, and she was simply thrilled to get it. She said we would paint the ceilings in our house. We had moved up from a big belly cold stove that burned coal to a gas furnace in the living room, and the ceilings did need to be painted. So one day, she got the paint and rollers brushes ready for us to paint, and we had two chairs, one for her and one for me. We got started, and the paint was like water. It didn't have much color of white at all, so she stirred and stirred and seemed not to help, but we started trying to roll in on the ceiling, and it would not cover at all. She told me to keep putting coats on that we had plenty of paint, and keep in mind, I did not know what I was doing and had never painted before ever. However, I sure was trying hard to please my mother.

I wanted the room to look nice for her. I guess she had just gotten so upset about the paint, and it was not working. She would have been sixty years old at that time, and remember I was her tenth child.

I said to my mommy, "This is not working. It is like water."

She turned around in her chair on the other side of the room and threw her paint roller, and I was not completely sure if she was aiming for me or maybe just so frustrated she cracked, but it came right at me, and she screamed loud at me. About the time, it hit me right in the stomach and knocked me off the chair, falling to the floor. She was furious. She was just so upset, but it wasn't my fault that the paint was not made to put inside the house. She stormed outside, not checking to see if I was alive or dead on the floor. My mother tried so hard to make things look nice, and it was so difficult. Nothing more was said, and we didn't get our ceiling painted.

Looking back, I understand how she must have felt, knowing it was not working, and the hurt she must have had. I blamed her son-in-law for the mess we were in. He must have known this kind of paint might not work indoors but thought it was a good gesture to bring to her. I remember she used it on some old metal furniture outside, and it worked okay. She was pleased with that.

Later I think she felt bad about hurting me, or maybe she didn't. I didn't think she had ever or would never forgive me for breaking up with Lynn. I felt she thought I had missed out on a good life. She had not given me a chance to grow and see for myself. I was still only fifteen, and school was about to begin and another year to experience. She was now sixty years old and still raising a teenager, but I was a good kid. I never gave her reason to worry about me. I honestly think she thought of me as a grandchild, or so that was how I was treated.

But I didn't think that really mattered because she had raised kids since she was seventeen years old and had a very hard life. I had never seen or known anyone so strong as she, and to this day, no one comes close. I asked her once, "Why have you not left my dad if he didn't help you?"

She said, "Honey, I did a time or two, and he could come to get me."

I also asked her, "Why have so many kids. You have ten children. How do you afford that if you don't have help?"

She said, "That's just the way it was meant to be." She sure loved her children. I guess she had her favorites, of course, and I certainly was not one of them, but that was okay. I knew in my heart, I was going to be my own special person, didn't know when and how, but I just could feel it. I feel it's a privilege to be the tenth child in this family because there is a reason. I believe for everything that happens, and Lord knows what that reason was for me.

My eleventh year of school was difficult. My older sister Jean had to have surgery, and my mom had to go stay with her for eight weeks, and she left me with my older brother. He had two boys, age six and seven, I loved them, but they only had two bedrooms, and it made it hard for them to find a space for me, but they did. I rarely see my brother Frank. He would be gone to work when I got ready for school and would be late coming home in the evenings. I had lots of time to think about things and got lonely quite often. I would walk up in the hollow where we used to live. My mom rented our old house, and my sister lived just below that house so I would go visit her and play with her baby boy. He was two and I loved him so much and he loved me. We had a special bond. I missed Noah and the fun times he and I had, and I missed Jenny. They had moved away to another state, and my heart was so lonely. I just felt like I didn't have anyone to talk to about things going on in my life. I did miss my mom, but I was used to her being gone and away from me. I was restless and really was having a difficult time.

After a couple of weeks went by, I asked if I could go stay with another brother, Robert, who lived down on the main highway, and they said yes. He had one son, who was about five years old, and a baby girl. I got to see him more often and didn't get as lonely. I also had a good school friend who lived in the same area that I could walk to her house, and that was fun time for me. Robert would be up fixing his lunch when I was ready for school, he would have a stack of sandwiches of eight or more, and I asked him, "Do you feed all the workers at your job?"

my brother Robert and me

He would just laugh and say, "No, those are for me," and he said, "Your big brother works hard and gets hungry." He was a big guy, and I loved him much. He was a jolly soul and a great man.

I started going out with some friends on the weekends, no boys but just friends who were older than me and could drive and had their own cars. We would just drive around and go eat, and they would talk to guys. I was very shy and would stay quiet. After a couple of trips, my brother Robert sat me down and said that he did not want me going out anymore, that he did not want me to get a bad name.

I said, "Why do you think I would get a bad name?"

"Who you hang out with and run around with will be how others will look and judge you, and you are a good girl, and you need to stay that way."

So I did not go out anymore with those friends. I stayed a couple more weeks with him and was glad he took time to talk to me, and I listened. Then I went to a friend's house when her mom invited me to stay a few days.

It was a very long year. I was fifteen now and had gone through a growth spurt and was taller than anyone else in my friend group.

My mom finally came home after I ended up staying a few days with my friend's house. I ended up at three households while my mom was off helping Jean. It was a lonely time for me.

She was back, and my brother Matt came back home from being away for a while and brought a girlfriend home with him. By now, school was about done, and I had almost made it through the year. I felt this was not going to be good, and I was right. We were back where we were when we had to leave and go move in with my sister Lou. He was worse now. He would talk awfully to his girlfriend and my mom. He would drink all the time when he would pass out. My mom and I would look for his beer and whiskey, and she would pour it out, and oh boy, when he came to and realized his stuff was missing, he would throw things and curse us all out and threaten to kill us all. I was so afraid, and in those moments, I wished I had gotten married to Lynn like my mom wanted me to and wondered what life I could have had. I was kept full of fear and still having to go and try to do my schoolwork. I couldn't concentrate on anything because I was sure he would kill us through the night, and I could not sleep, and again I had to be so quiet so he could sleep in the mornings. I could not understand why the rest of my mom's children allowed this. He was now twenty years old, and my mom could not do anything with him when he was sixteen, and surely, she could not do anything now. But we had a family of ten with me the youngest and him next to me in age five years apart. It was strange this happened to him. What went wrong? I still don't know, but I think about it and speculate.

He finally left after about a month or two, and it was just Mom and me. We would hear stuff through the night, and she would think someone was trying to break in on us. We would get out at midnight and walk over to my brother's house and stay till morning, then come back, and I would get ready for school.

The school year in tenth grade was ending. I had made it and was glad the year was over. Summer was here, and my mom and I got on the Greyhound bus and would go visit my sisters. My niece Jenny was getting married, and we went to her wedding that summer. I cried at her wedding. She was so very beautiful. She was seventeen, and I was thinking that could have been me right now at fifteen, and I was so torn on whether I had made a mistake or not in my life, and Jenny's marriage did not work out, but she had a beautiful daughter. Jenny and I would always stay close with great memories of my happy times visiting her and my nephew, Noah, and memories of growing up and riding bikes up the highway, go exploring, trying and finding grapevines like we did when we were little kids, just fun stuff that we enjoyed doing.

Their mom had four kids of her own now from five to seventeen. My sister Ally had five kids, ages three to ten. Each sister would go on to have another kid each.

We had our visit, and my mom would stay if we could because she was afraid my brother would come back home if he knew we were there, so we could see peace during the summer.

Time passed quickly, and it was time to go, and we would go to the bus station and ride the big Greyhound bus back home. I remember I would leave with tears on my face; I did not want to go home. School time was coming, and I would go into the eleventh grade. I was simply amazed. I had made it this far being sad lots of my time but trying to remember there had to be good things ahead in life for me. I was hanging on to faith in my heart.

My mom would take me to town and buy me new shoes at the little shoe store across the bridge in town and get me a new piece of clothing. She did not have much money, but she had more than she did when my father was still living.

On my first day of eleventh grade, I had my new shoes and outfit. I was ready, got my classes, knew where I was to be, and another year was up and running. I had to borrow a lot of clothes from my friends, and I had gone through a growth spurt and gotten much taller than them. So many dresses were very short but so was everyone else's, and I didn't think much about it. However, we did have a dress code at school that our dresses were supposed to be a certain length, but no one was ever there, well, except a few. I loved pretty clothes, and I didn't have much, but I made do with what I had and could borrow. From time to time, I would get called to the office about my miniskirts, and I would say, "This is all I have to wear."

So the principal would say, "If I send you home, are you saying you don't have anything else to wear more appropriate?"

I would say, "No, sir. And anyway, I don't have anyone to come get me. No one has a car at my home."

He usually just shook his head and told me to get some new clothes. I would tell him we had no money, and that would probably not happen.

August and September passed, and I turned sweet sixteen with no big deal, no celebration, cake, or balloons, but I was okay. I was sixteen. I was surely grown now and on my way. I felt I was truly a miracle. I would have hoped some of my family would have wished me a happy birthday on this day. In my heart, I rejoiced and probably thanked God for getting me this far.

It was beginning to be a bad winter. It was the end of October, and we already had snow, and it was getting very cold. My friend was running for homecoming queen; she had it all, looks, money, and a good family, one who helped me through so far. I borrowed her clothes, and her mom was part of the reason for my eight-grade trip to Washington, DC, and I loved them for that. She had a dance at the grade school to raise money for her title. The most money got you the title of homecoming queen. I wanted to go to this dance so bad because I had a huge crush on one of the basketball players. He was the star of the game, and I thought he liked me too. He was going to be there, so I begged my mom to let me go, and she finally did, but my brother Matt was back and he was throwing a fit, telling her not to allow me to go. I was too young to be going to a dance; however, I told him I would do whatever he wanted me to do if he would just let it go, that I was now sixteen years old, and so he said, "I will not carry in any coal. You will do it all."

I said, "Fine. I always do it anyway."

So that night, I was thrilled to get to have some fun time. That night was fun; we all danced. The boy I had a crush on was there, and we talked. I was very nervous. I had not been out with anyone since

I broke up with my boyfriend, Lynn. I had only been treated like a princess and lightly kissed and had my hand held gently with love. No parts of my body other than my lips and hands had ever been touched. I had been totally treated with care by a gentleman. So that was what I expected even having a huge crush on this guy. We were sitting at a table, and he leaned over and kissed me on the mouth. It felt great.

He asked, "Can I take you home?"

I said, "Yes."

He took my hand and held it gently and said, "I have wanted to ask you out for a while now," and I just smiled at him. After the dance was over, we left, and my house was not far in the hollow.

As we were pulling up, he said, "Can we sit out here and talk?"

As I was going to say, "Yes, we can do that," I heard Matt yelling inside the house, and it scared me so much that he would come out and make a seen. So I told him I was sorry but had to go on in the house.

He looked at me and said, "Did I do something wrong?"

I said, "No, I just have to go." I was too embarrassed to tell him I had a twenty-one-year-old brother who was an alcoholic and on drugs and caused me trouble. He left, and we never went out or got together after that, but I always cherished that kiss.

Again it had gotten so bad. My mom said we would have to leave and go back to live with my sister Lou. I was so upset, wondering again if I should just drop out of school. How could anyone continue to live like this and try to get through high school? So again, I started in January for the last semester of my eleventh year. I had gotten to know several kids over the years, coming and going, and they remembered me. I still had to walk to and from school because I had found out there was no bus that went to where I lived, so I had to walk or get a ride. I often wondered why I had to live like this and have such a hard time trying to go to school. It was hard changing schools and different classes. Still a lot of kids were bullies and would laugh at me and stare at me in class. I was a hillbilly they said, and I guess I was not really knowing just what that even meant at that time. I was not up for arguing or fighting with anyone. I wanted a peaceful, safe life. But keeping in my heart the faith that someday surely life would be better. I would go home in the evening and play with the baby. She was about ten months old and was like her big sister, just beautiful. When I would wake up in the mornings, her dad would come in to make sure I was awake for school, and the baby would be standing up in her baby bed, looking at me. I would sit her out each morning, and she would crawl around behind me while I got ready for school. She did this every day. In the evenings, I would stop at the store and get her candy my sister said it was okay, and I could get her whatever I wanted if it was not hard candy. I didn't know much about babies at all; I just loved them. I played with them the remaining year, and it gave me something to look forward to going home in the evening. I had a couple of dates, but nothing good came of them. One guy I went on a date with had a dash full of marijuana smokers, and I was scared the entire date and very glad to get home because I did not drink or do any type of drugs.

Winter seemed long and hard. I had to walk to and from school almost every day. Sometimes I got so cold I felt numb, but I made it, and summer was here, and school was almost out. I still thought of my first and really the only boyfriend I had and still missed him. I just knew if he were here, my life would be so much easier and better, but he had moved away with a broken heart, and I felt sad for him. My mind would tell me that he was not meant to be, but I was so very thankful God had put him in my life at an early age, and I knew I was here for another time and another life that would be good for me. I just needed to grow up and survive all the things I had gone through. I had again made it through another semester of school and was going to be a senior in high school in the fall. Summer was here. Thank you, Lord. We were on our way home. I was sad to leave those sweet kids but knew they needed their room back as sisters.

I thought, *Lord, will I have to do this again in my last year of school?* But I quickly took the idea out of my head and tried to focus on having a good summer I deserved it.

My mom was starting to say harsh things to me; it was like she just decided to take a look at me now like she never had before, and she would say that I was getting too tall as I had passed her years earlier. She was a petite woman, and I was not going to be that. I had also passed my friends in height and was two to three or more inches taller than all of them, but that was okay with me.

I would go out with some friends and meet boys, but they were a little too wild for me, and I didn't like the way they acted, and I didn't think they knew how to treat a girl. However, I did meet one guy, and he was very nice to me and treated me respectfully, and I dated him for a while until school started, and it was over, but he was okay. I struggled with shy issues and did not have confidence, but I knew I was strong and would make it through whatever came at me.

Summer went by quickly, and school was coming up soon. I didn't know where I would be going as my brother was still a problem. He had gone to live with my older brother for a while, and it didn't work out, then with my older sister Ally again, but it didn't work out. He just seemed not to be able to get his life on track to ever have a good life. Finally, my senior year of school was here. I thought to myself, *This is going to be my best year!* I almost made it. My mom took me into town shopping and bought me a very cute outfit. I could not wear it to school; it was very short with matching bloomers. I loved it. We also got a new pair of shoes for me from a regular shoe store that had all new shoes, not the little store across the bridge that sold used shoes although I love the loafers I always got there, and so I felt I was ready to go.

My mom said, "I don't know if we can stay here this year for you to graduate."

I replied, "Mommy, I have to stay here to graduate, or I will have to quit. I don't think I can take another split year. Just please leave me with anyone and let me finish if you must go, I understand."

She looked sad, kind of like if you had kept your boyfriend, you would be married now, and he would take care of us. Or that was what I was thinking her thoughts just might be.

71

I felt so sorry for her. She had not had much of a life at all raising ten kids and having so much trouble with Matt. She surely did
not deserve it. My job, I thought, was to not give her any reason to
worry about me, and I didn't think I ever did. She had been different
toward me since my breakup. I really knew in my heart that her heart
had been broken more than mine, and there was nothing I could do.
I would feel overwhelmed with guilt from time to time that I let her
down by not getting married and making a good life for her.

The first day of the senior year arrived, and off I went had to
walk down the road up the little hill and stand by the bus stop that I
had stood at many years before from time to time. I was excited. We
now were the older ones on the bus, and of course, the little freshman
class would be intimidated by us, but we would be sweet and nice
to them getting to school, going to my classes, and seeing familiar
faces. They seemed to be glad I was back. I saw my basketball star in
the hallway with another girl, but he still gave me a look as he would
rather be with me. This was a new year, the last year of high school,
and I wanted to make the best of it. We had to go to the vocational
technical college the second half of the day every day for business
and office. I enjoyed learning computer and typing; I was good at it.

The bus would run, but we always got a ride with one of the
boys who had a new car and drove to school. He became an awesome
friend. He would make a detour and go through Jerry's and get us all
a Jboy box to eat on the way to school. It was so cool to be friends
with him, and sometimes we did play hooky and go into town and
hang out until time to go back and catch our bus home. No one
usually found out. After a couple of weeks of school, one guy came
up to me in the hallway and asked if I wanted to go on a date with a
friend of his from vo-tech school. I said to show him to me tomorrow, and he did, and I said, "No, thanks," because I didn't think he
was good-looking.

He said, "Please go out with him. He really likes you," and he
said, "I want to go out with your friend."

I said no again.

Every day, he would come to me in the hallway and keep asking me to go out, and I would keep saying no. I had not had much luck with a boyfriend since my breakup with Lynn. No one could ever match up to him and the way he treated me. There was no interest for me at this time. I just wanted to enjoy where I was and hang out with my friends. It was labor day weekend, and my friend and I were home with no date, and her phone rang, and it was the guy from school, and he said, "Would you go out if I could get another guy?"

I said, "Maybe, and who would it be?"

"My brother."

I thought, "Oh no, is he going to be annoying like you?"

My friend and I talked and said, "Well, we have no date, and at least we could get to go to the movies or something." So we said okay, and the date and time was set.

We got ready, went to my house, and of course, my brother Matt was there, acting crazy as usual, and wanted to know where we thought we were going, and I told him we were just going out with some friends. My mom was okay with us going. He had been drinking heavilyy I could tell, and it was going to a big worry for me and another embarrassing time. We heard the guys coming, and I had not met or seen my date, but it was Saturday night, and I had not been out or really had any fun, so I was excited.

As they were coming up the dirt road, we were watching, and about the time the car pulled in front of the house, my brother Matt ran out the back kitchen door unto the road by our house, yelling with a shotgun in his hand, saying he was going to hurt a neighbor man who lived up in the hollow. It scared and embarrassed me so bad I almost threw up. We hurried to get in the car, didn't even have them come in the house, and they said, "Who was that guy with a gun?"

I said, "My brother." That was all that was said that night about him. I worried for Matt and leaving as my mom was yelling at him to come back. My thoughts were *what would happen* and *if mom would be ok*ay. How was I going to enjoy this date? However, I was totally shocked at the looks of this guy I was set up with. He was a beautiful man, long hair down around his neck and perfect. So I just felt and knew I didn't have a chance here, so I just went with it and figured a movie and popcorn would be good.

As we were going down the road, he started talking about his girlfriend. She had something to do tonight, and he thought he would come with his brother, and I thought, *Fellow, if you think this is bothering me, it's not.* I didn't say anything other than just sit there and allow him to talk. This guy has a girlfriend, and of course, I had no shot here at all, and it was fine with me because I thought who comes to take a girl out and talks about his girlfriend, and that threw me off completely because I deserve more much more.

We got to the movies and pulled in, and my friend said, "Let's go to the restroom," and we got out. She was dying. She said, "OMG! He is the cutest guy I ever saw," and I said, "Yes, but he has a girlfriend. Did you not hear him talking about her the whole way to the movies?"

"Yes, but I don't care. What are you going to do?"

I said, "Nothing at all, just enjoy the movies." I was not interested in a guy like this. He was gorgeous, and he knew it. I was no match for him, and he was no match for me.

We went back to the car, and as I sat on my side of the car, he had bucket seats, and there was a big console in the middle. He asked me if I was shy and if I didn't want to move closer to him, and I said, "No, I am okay where I am."

He left the car, and in a few minutes, he came back with popcorn and a Coke for me. I said, "Thank you." He moved over and out his arm around me. As I was getting very nervous, I thought to myself, *You are such a creep, cheating on your girlfriend,* and he said he had dated her for three years. Like who does that? So really, I was not interested at all. So when he reached down and put a big lip lock on me, I guess I kind of felt something, but I was not going to allow it because it was not acceptable. His girlfriend was out of town or something, and here he was with me now. What does that say about character? So I quickly pulled away, and he asked why.

I said to him, "I wonder what your girlfriend would think of you kissing another girl?" and that I just wanted to watch the movie.

I thought it shocked him a little by the look on his face. I was not easy, never had been, and by now, it was never going to happen. His brother and my friend were in the back seat; they seemed to be enjoying themselves.

I think my friend wished she was where I was. She was the one who usually got all the cute boys. This time, it was me, and I didn't appear to want him. We did have a couple more kisses just so, I guess, I could brag the next day, kissing a beautiful guy, and then was time to go home. I prayed my brother Matt was not out with that shotgun because I do believe he could really hurt someone when he is drunk or high on drugs. There was no sign of Matt, and I stayed over with my friend, and she lived farther up the hollow. When we got out, he asked me if I was going to call him, and I said no, and he looked kind of funny and said, "Why not?"

I said, "You have a girlfriend, so you should be nice to her."

My friend was like "Are you crazy? He is too cute. I would call him."

I said, "Well, I am not and don't want to. I'm just not interested in that kind of guy, but he sure could kiss good, and I did feel something I had not felt before, but of course, I had not had much experience at all."

She and I talked into the night about him. She didn't have much to say about her date who was his brother she was with, but he seemed like a nice enough guy. I had my eye on another guy whom I liked. However, the week passed, and on Thursday, JM called me and asked if I knew who he was. I said no, knowing exactly who it was, and he said, "Have you missed me?"

I said, "Who is this?"

"JM."

"No."

"You haven't thought about me one time?"

"No, sure haven't."

"Well, I have been thinking about you, and would you like to go out tomorrow night?"

Tomorrow would have been Friday, and I said, "No."

"Why?"

"I am going to the ball game with my friends."

"What about Saturday?"

"I doubt it."

"Can I call you back?"

"Why are you even calling me? It's not like we had a really great time on our date."

"I'm sorry. I guess I talk too much about my girlfriend."

"Well, you should be calling and talking with her."

Not much more was said, and then that call was quickly forgotten. I was thinking to myself, *If he thinks I'm easy for him, he has another thought coming.*

I told my friend, and she was like, "Are you crazy? I will go out with him."

I said, "Well, go on because I am not interested. I am looking for more, not someone who is a cheater."

So we went to the ball game and had a really good time, and the guy I liked wanted to take me home, and my friend said she didn't want to ride the bus without me and just to tell him I was going to ride the bus. I surely didn't want to for sure, but I did because I was a much better friend to my friends than my friends were to me. It had always been like that, and I think still to this day that's true.

Around eleven that night, the phone rang. We were in bed, and my mom answered the phone as it scared her that late at night, and I heard her say, "Who is this?" She came and said, "It's for you. Make sure you tell him not to call here this late at night ever again," and I did. It was JM.

He said, "Do you know who this is?"

I said, "Yes, because you told my mom." I thought, *Well, he's not only a cheater but a little goofy too.* I was still sad and a little upset that the guy from school I liked didn't get to bring me home.

I said, "So what do you want?"

"My brother told on you."

"What?"

He went on to say his brother saw me talking to another guy, and I said, "Yes, he was going to bring me home, but we rode the bus."

"That is good."

I kept thinking about what this guy's deal. He was dating a girl for three years, and why was he calling me? Did he think he could take advantage of me? I was a good girl and was going to stay that way. I had been around one or two guys like that, and I could hold my own and move on because I knew someone would be there someday who could match up to how Lynn treated me, and I was determined not to settle for anything less.

He said, "So are you going to go out with me tomorrow night?"

I said, "No, why would you think I would? What about your girlfriend?"

"We broke up last night."

I felt he was lying just to get me out, so I said, "Maybe, only if my friend and your brother go back out, and I'm not sure she wants to go back out with him."

He said he would have him check with her. He again apologized for talking so much about his girlfriend on our date.

So Saturday came, and my friend was excited to be going out again, not sure if it was because of JM's brother or him. They picked us up again at my house, and Matt was still home being his usual self, but we made it to the car, and as we were going down the road, we talked a little about our day and how school was going for me so far. We went to a big field where lots of young kids would go park, get out, sit on the ground, and talk, so that's what we did. It was the second date on Saturday night, same night last week we went to movies. We parked, and my friend and his brother got out, and the first thing he said was, "Why don't you like me?"

I said, "I don't know you, and all you talked about last weekend was your girlfriend. I think you are a cheater, and who would like someone like that? Certainly not me."

He had beautiful teeth and would smile big at me like he was amazed by me, kind of like my very first boyfriend did when I was fourteen. I was now sixteen, and in a month, I would be seventeen. I had grown up fast, but that first boyfriend had left me to have very high expectations in a guy. He pulled me close to him and said it was not working out with the girl he had been dating for three years, and the proof for him was going out with me. He had broken up with her last night, and I felt sadness over me for her.

I said, "I hope it's not because of me."

"You are nothing like any girl I have ever taken out."

"How? Because I didn't fall all over you and act like a silly love-sick girl?"

"No, that was not."

I was just different, and he really liked me, so it softened me up a little but not much.

So he said, "Do you think I can pick you up at school and take you home next week?"

"Maybe, I will think about it."

After I got home, I thought maybe he wanted me alone so he could take advantage of me. He could certainly have any girl he wanted. He was so cute, had a sharp car, so what was the deal here? I was not a beauty, but I was not ugly either. I was caught somewhere in the middle, I guess. So I said no that week and did not allow him to pick me up. All the girls at school were talking. My friend had told them all about him, and she was like, "He is so cute." I couldn't figure out why he didn't want to go out with her. She got all the cool and good-looking guys.

The next week, we were all out by the school, waiting to get on the bus, and he pulled that sharp car around, and the window was down, and he said, "Can I give you a ride home?"

My heart started pounding like it was going to come out of my chest, and I was really nervous, thinking what should I do, and my friend said, "You are not going to go, are you?"

My other friends said, "Wow. He is so cute. Yes, you have to go."

Standing there, awkward, I kind of shook my head and walk toward his car and got in, and he said, "How was your day?"

I said, "Okay, I guess."

He reached over and took my hand, and I could tell I was blushing. I could feel my body starting to sweat, and that just never happened. I thought he would think I like him, and I didn't know if I did or not. It was too early for me to decide. I had to see more proof.

We never said anything more until we were closer to my house, and he said, "Do you want me to pick you up again tomorrow?"

"I don't know."

"Ask your mom and see if she will allow you to go eat or something before I bring you home."

I was very worried Matt would be out and see us coming up the road and start trouble, so I had my plan to jump out of the car and hurry him off, and that was what I did. That night, he called me and asked if my mom said it's okay for him to pick me up again.

I told him, "I did not ask her, but I might ask in the morning."

"How will I know to pick you up?"

"You won't. You will just have to drive by and see."

The next day at school, the girls were all gathering around the locker to see how the ride home went, and I told them he just took me home, and I got out, and that was it. That evening came, and I was excited about if he was going to be coming up that hill and really didn't know why because I still like the other guy more. Class and the day were over, and we all rushed out to wait for the bus. Usually it was not there yet, and guess who was there waiting on me? JM. I could feel myself feeling proud and beaming because the other girls were giggling, and away I went to his car and got in.

He said, "Can you stay out a little while this evening?"

"Just for about an hour or so."

He smiled a big smile at me with those beautiful white teeth and took my hand in his. I was thinking this guy has got it bad, or else he was wanting something from me. I was not going to give him. We went through Jerry's and got food and sat there, ate, and talked. He told me more about himself, like working for his dad through the summer to get the car he was driving, and this was not his first car, and that he had worked out every car he had so far. Once he said he went to Chicago and worked on the railroad for a summer to buy a car and his school clothes. He said it had been a long time since his mother had to buy him anything. That was very impressive to me. My thoughts started changing about him that day. He was very gentle and so respectful.

I had seen his girlfriend downtown. A few weeks later, my friend and I were playing hooky from class, and she was so beautiful with long blond hair and very petite. I was tall and had shoulder-length brown hair. There was no comparison in looks, so I thought at that time, I better not let my guard down for a second. Why would he break up with her after three years? And there had been talk of marriage for the two of them.

Every weekend after that, we went out most times with other friends and would have a great time. My birthday came in October, and I turned seventeen. He took me out to dinner and brought me a rose. He had fallen hard within the next month, and he asked me to marry him. I told him we had only known each other for two months, and he said he knew I should be with him. During this time, I was having trouble with his prior girlfriend and her older sisters. They would call me names and say I took him away, and I would say, "Oh no, I did not," and try to explain, but they were furious. I knew I had not done anything. It was very hard dealing with that girl's whole family. I really felt sorry and bad for her. She truly loved him, it appeared.

My senior year of school was my best by far. My brother Matt would be in and out with his girlfriends and make trouble, but we were getting by. I could tell my mom was troubled by me going out each weekend with my now new boyfriend, but she never said much about it. My sisters would have boyfriends visit and be at my mom's when I would come home from dates. I always was home by eleven, and sometimes they would try and get me in trouble. It was funny because they were the older ones with kids that should have been in trouble.

Christmas was coming up, and I didn't have any money, but I had been working on a school program for poor kids to earn money.

Some of us stayed after school and cleaned the vocational-technical college building where we had classed half of each day.

I took some of my money and bought my boyfriend a sweater. He liked the blue and gold. My friend was still dating his brother, and our school colors were red and white, so we switched colors because she wanted to get the blue and gold and said we should not get the same colors, so I got red and white. They had the same initials.

I wondered about that later and had my suspicions on the reason why. But it was okay. He loved his present, and I didn't think it would have mattered what I got him. He didn't expect anything from me. He wanted to do everything for me, it seemed. His present to me was a pearl ring and said we should get married in January, and I asked about school, and he said, "You will finish, and we can get an apartment."

I thought, "No, there is no hurry. We have plenty of time."

Little did I know at that time, we were already slipping into a timeless love story. So every time we would go out, and that would be every weekend, he would ask when I was going to marry him, and I would reply, "You don't have a job, and I am not ready to get married." Yet I didn't even know if I was in love. I was just enjoying my time. I was not having to live in another state for the first time in three years and walking to school in blizzard-type weather. I was having fun for the first time in school and in life.

Although my brother Matt was still an issue for my mom and me, she was handling it well. I was wearing my little pearl ring in style on one hand and his class ring on the other hand. I was doing fine. Time went by quickly, and prom was coming soon. I had never gotten to go to the prom and was nervous but excited. Also, my mom took me to town, and in a little dress shop, I found the perfect gown for me. It was deep purple with a slit all way down the front of the dress with silver sequins trimmed. It fit me great, and then she took me and got shoes to match. I felt like a princess. I was very thankful, and I wondered how she got the money or if she could have to use the money for something she needed. Nothing was ever said about it. I got ready that night, and he picked me up, and I remember the neighbor who lived across the road from us came down about the time we were getting in his car and said, "You sure do look awful pretty."

I said, "Thank you," and blushed because my mom did not tell me I look pretty. I think that would have meant a lot to me.

We went to the prom, and everyone looked so beautiful and was getting pictures made. We did not want to stand in line, and he said, "We will come back." However, by the time we went back, they had quit taking pictures, and I didn't get to have one. I was sad, of course, and no one had brought a camera with them, so I had to just sketch a memory in time in my mind on that night so I would never forget it. By then, he was so in love he couldn't quit thinking about us being together all the time, and I would keep reminding him how young I was, and there was plenty of time. He was such a gentleman and treated me so good, always easy on the kisses, and hands stayed where they should have just like my first boyfriend. I had so I knew he was a keeper but just not so fast. I loved him, but graduation was coming up next, and he would say, "Let's elope and get married right after graduation."

I said, "I am not old enough. You have to be eighteen, and that's months away."

My graduation picture

There had been times that I had concerns and doubts about graduating. I would be the second of ten children to finish high school in my family. I had been determined to make it, but the chances seemed not so good for me. I had studied hard, and through it all, I had made it by faith and grace, and I knew that in my heart.

Graduation day was here. My boyfriend's family all came, and my friend's mom picked up my mom, so she could come to watch. They brought me gifts and gave me hugs. I felt very proud that day for my mom and me. I didn't graduate top in my class, but I was not on the bottom either, so I was proud of what I had gone through to get here. When my name was called, it was second to the last name called out of over two hundred students because they went in alphabetical order. I know I was beaming with pride. I had made it and got my diploma. What an accomplishment for me. I had made it through almost seventeen years with much difficulty and had never had a thought of turning to drugs or alcohol although it had been offered to me multiple times. I was thankful to be in this school and for my group of students, many who would remain my friends through life. We visited with a few people and then was on our way back home.

When we got back home, my mom said, "Are you ready to go on a trip?"

I said, "Well, my boyfriend wants me to marry him, Mom, and I told him we could wait a while but maybe not for long."

She looked at me in a funny sort of way and said, "I don't think you should marry him. I have heard a few things about his family," and went on to say that we should go away awhile and see how this works out.

So I said, "Well, okay." I never did anything intentionally to upset my mom or do anything disrespectful to her. I was a good girl and tried hard to make things easy for her.

Our first trip that summer was to my aunt Ethel's house about two hours away. When I told JM we were going away to do visits with our family, he said, "Let me take you and your mom," so I thought this would help my mom get to know him better and see if he was a genuine good guy, and my mom was grateful for him to take us. I could tell it was hard for him to leave me, and he stayed if he could. One good thing that happened here was my aunt liked him, and I was glad. We stayed there for a few days and then got a Greyhound bus and went on to visit my sister whom I had lived with my prior years. I was missing JM already very much. We stayed there for most of the summer, and my sister was trying to fix me up with different guys, and there were always people at her house, but I was not interested at all because now I knew where my heart was and belonged to, so I would walk to the neighborhood phone booth and call JM. I could hear the excitement in his voice just to hear from me, and he would say, "Come home and marry me. I have a good job and can take care of you."

I replied, "I don't know when we are coming back. What if my mom wants us to stay here and live?"

He said, "I will come and get you."

As time passed, I missed him so much and put more thought in my mind that this was truly real, and he loved me as much or more than my first boyfriend Lynn. Who could find love like that twice? Now I was old enough to know; I would be eighteen in a few months.

My mom seemed determined to change my mind somehow. She even had my sister's friend talk to me about getting married. He said he would marry me and take good care of me. He was much older and a good guy, of course, but I had known him and his wife when I was in school here. His wife had left him for another man he said and was heartbroken. I felt bad for him, but that was it. There was no way I would let this happen. Why would my mom want another older man to marry me just to take care of me? I thought this was very strange, and it dawned on me what was happening. She wanted to make sure I was secure, so she would not have to worry about me, not that she ever did. Maybe so she could have a safe place to come to, but she could have that with JM and me. It was now the end of July, and I asked my mom if we could go home. I knew where I wanted to be.

Reluctantly she agreed to bring me home. We got on the Greyhound bus, and arriving home, I was so excited to see my guy, but he was even more excited to see me.

He said, "I was getting ready to come up there and get you and bring you home with me."

JM and me

August was here. He had a good job, and I decided to marry him the next month in September, and his brother and my friend, who were dating, were going with us. I even thought maybe they would get married also. They had dated for almost a year also. The day in September came. My mom was very quiet and didn't offer to help me get ready, but my sister-in-law came over and helped me. I felt a little alone but knew this was what I wanted, and I had an inner excitement that was stronger than my loneliness. My mom had to go to the courthouse and sign for me to marry because I was not yet eighteen, so I had to ensure I took those papers with me. I was surprised on the day she went and signed maybe proved she wanted me to be happy. I asked her if she wanted to go with us to get married, and she shook her head no with her back to me. There was no big wedding planned for me by no one. At the last minute, his brother and my friend decided not to go and be our witness. They maybe had fought over something, and my heart felt a little sad as I was looking forward to the four of us doing this together. We had to take two witnesses with us, or we thought we did, so his mother and grandmother went. I was even sadder that this happened, and my mom didn't even want to go. I was so torn and even cried. The car was very quiet on the three-hour drive, and JM would hold and squeeze my hand and whisper how much he loved me and couldn't wait for me to be his wife. We went to another state and found a church with a pastor. He was a wonderful pastor, and his wife was there with him. He looked over the paper my mom had signed and spoke with us about marriage. We were both nervous and anxious at the same time. I wondered in that moment why I didn't just wait until I turned eighteen as it was only a month away. They say love can wait, but sometimes I guess it can't.

He took us up front of the beautiful church and said, "Now we will take pictures," and no one had a camera. I did not have a camera, and his mother or grandmother hadn't thought to bring one. He said he was sorry that we could not get to have any pictures of our wonderful day. But we knew we would always have the picture in our minds of our beautiful day. He proceeded with our ceremony, and finally, after a year of dating and finding the true love of my life, I was a married young lady of seventeen. On the way home, it was still quiet, but his mother and grandmother spoke often, and his mother said, "JM, your father is going to throw a fit over this," and it kind of hurt my feelings as to why he would throw a fit. JM was twenty years old and had a job and had not lived at home in years. He lived with his grandmother and had always worked through the summers and bought his own car and his clothes to wear to school. JM just reached over and took my hand in his and looked at me and smiled. We stopped at a drive-through restaurant and got chicken to eat. I could hardly eat anything because I was so nervous. We got back and took his mother and grandmother home, and sure enough, his father was home, and when we went in, his brother had already told his dad we went to get married. The first words that came out of his mouth was "What have you done, son?"

JM looked at him and said, "I am married to the girl of my dreams, Dad."

Nothing more was said, and we left. He had gotten a hotel room that night for our honeymoon. I had never stayed in a hotel before, so this was a big deal in every way.

He had already rented an apartment and had everything in place for us. We took our packed-up clothes and moved into our apartment. I loved it.

He said to me when we went inside, "Know this that I love you more than life itself and will always take care of you, and you can count on me always."

I could feel myself blush as I was so in love with this beautiful man. What had I ever done to deserve this? And whatever it was, I was so very thankful.

visiting my mom

Living in an apartment was fun. It was very nice. JM would get up and go to work early, and I would be by myself and would work in the apartment, cleaning and making everything look pretty. I would wait patiently for him to get home from work and was so excited to see him. We were so much in love, and I was finally complete. Our first trip to the grocery store was too funny. We neither knew what to buy, and we came out with a box of spaghetti to make for that evening, and we did. Of course, we could not eat it. Something had gone wrong in the preparation. My mother-in-law happened to stop by and check on us. She could see what mess we had made, and she said, "What else do you have to fix?"

We said, "This is all we got."

She laughed and took us back to the grocery and taught us how to shop. We had a lot of stuff to fix, and she gave me pointers on how to make dinner.

I did not have my driver's license yet but did have my permit. I wasn't supposed to drive without a driver's license with me, but after a week went by, I wanted to go see my mom, so after JM left for work off, I went to spend the day with my mom. There was a shortcut across the mountain that I would take to stay off the main highway, and I did this every week, and my mom was always glad to see me.

Most of the time, I would eat with my mom and she would send stuff back with me and sometimes she would come over and cook. I think she was getting used to me being gone, but I wanted her to know I was here for her and would make sure she was okay. She never asked how I was doing or if I was happy. I could still see some sadness in her eyes. I wanted her to spend as much time with us as she could. I wanted her to have a better life that she deserved. Matt had still been a problem, but he was gone again for a short period. I think she knew he would be back soon.

One of my best friends was trying to help me parallel park downtown. I had to take my driving test, and I had to practice. I was having a hard time with parallel parking and knew I would fail my test again as this was what failed me before. My sister Lou took me for my driving test and the first thing I had to do was parallel park and I hit the curb and was an automatic failed test. So I needed a lot of practice. I thought I could do this, and about then, I backed into the parking meter and knocked it over, and she said she was not going with me again. I made her too nervous, and I didn't practice anymore for a while. I just drove with a permit. I figured the more I could drive, the better chance I would get my license.

I picked up another friend one day, and we went to the car wash to clean up our car. It was a blue convertible Mustang, such a sharp car, and I loved to drive it. We washed it and pulled it out to vacuum the inside. I had pulled up too far, and my friend was just learning how to drive, and I had already gotten out of the car, and my door was open. I realized I was up too far for the vacuum to reach, and I asked her to back it up just a little for me. She was thrilled to get in the driver's seat, and she backed up so fast, and the open door hit the vacuum post and came almost completely off. To say the least, it scared me so bad, but I was glad she was okay. I felt sick to my stomach. I had no license. Oh, what a day and what were we to do.

We walked over to the house across the street and asked if we could use the phone.

They said, "Is it a local call?"

I said, "Yes, it is." I called my friend Ben from school whose dad owned a body shop, and thank god, he was home. I said, "There is an accident with my car. Can you please come to us? I don't know what to do."

He came to us immediately, looked at the car, and said, "What happened?"

I told him, and he just shook his head and laughed a little. He worked on the door and got it to close enough to drive and took the car to his dad's shop after he dropped us off at the apartment and fixed it. You could hardly tell it had been damaged. He didn't charge anything for the labor, and I was so grateful to have such a good friend. The friend who did the damage was so sorry and felt awful about it, but I told her it was my fault for asking her to back up. It was several months before I told JM.

He said, "You can always tell me anything. It's okay. No one was hurt, but you are going to have to get your license." He took me out over the following weekend and taught me how to parallel park, and I went the next week and got my driver's license.

I continued to drive to my mom's almost every day of the week. Soon we moved from our cute apartment into a single-wide mobile home with a big porch built around, and we stayed there for the next few months. The lady we rented off asked me to babysit her two little girls while she was working, so I did for a couple of months. She paid me really good, and I liked having extra money, but I missed the freedom to go visit my mom every day. The kids were both good, but the youngest was not potty trained, and I hated that mess. Every morning, when I got there, the mom would leave, and I would have to change the messy diaper. I hated that, but I was getting paid, and it was a job.

We liked living in that little mobile home. One morning, I got up, and a pair of new pants that I had bought had been ripped to shreds. No one was there but me, and it scared me very badly.

I called my mom, and she said, "Honey, it sounds like you may have a rat."

"A rat?" I said. I had not been this scared in a long time as this was a different fear from what I felt in the past with Matt. I was trying to look around, and I didn't see anything at all. I put on some clothes and left and didn't go back in until JM got home. When I told him and showed him what happened, he said, "We must have a rat," and he said he would take care of it and set a trap. That night, he caught and disposed of it, and I felt he could do anything, and he did. I never heard or had that to happen again.

I had turned eighteen now and had finally grown up. I was settled, married, happy, graduated high school, survived by the grace of God, and thought I could change the world.

I was now going to look for a real job. I did not want to keep changing those messy diapers, and it did not appear she was going to potty train anytime soon. Some of my friends from school were in college now, and I would love to go, but not one teacher ever spoke to me about college, nor did anyone in my family. If they had, I would have been interested. However, that did not happen, and I went out determined to find a job, and the first place I stopped, I applied at the photo shop and got the job. How exciting! This was an important job. I would be the one developing the pictures. I was trained to work in the darkroom, and being so afraid of the dark since I was a kid, I thought this surely was a test for me, and something I would have to overcome to keep this job, and I was willing to try, and I became very good at it. I really enjoyed working at this job, but I missed going to visit my mom every day. I was making money and was still timid and shy but was getting a little better. I could now talk more to people. I had just got a little promotion and an increase in pay after a month of working, catching on fast, and then the unexpected happened.

JM's job ended, and my brother Robert said we should move to Lexington. That would be a good place for us to live, and I was okay with that because my aunt Ethel lived there, and I knew my mom could come down there often to stay with me and help her sister because her husband was sick. Everything was happening so fast. I really loved my job, and when I told my boss, he was very sad to see me go.

He said, "You will always be welcomed back if you are in need of a job if things don't work out where you are going."

I really appreciated that. My brother Robert got started quickly to find us an apartment, and JM had to find a job there. It never occurred to us for him to find a job here at home. There were plenty of jobs here, but I thought it was a way for my big brother to move us to a better place, and of course, Brother Zack, the one who taught me to ride a bike at four years old, was married now with a little daughter and lived there and was very happy to hear we might come to live there.

It was not taken very well with JM's family, but my mom was all in for us to go. I thought she wanted a good life for me, but I was sure there was nothing better than what I had now. I was in love, had a good job, and an awesome husband. What more could I ask for? A week went by, and my brother Robert called and said he was taking my husband to Lexington to find a job and said had a lead on the apartment and would check out when they got down there. The next day, they left and came back. He had a job, and we had a new apartment.

We got packed up. All we had were clothes and some dishes. I had given almost all the things I got at my bridal shower to my mom. There was so much, and I did not have enough space to put everything, and our mobile home was all furnished. I wanted my mom to have it all; she so deserved nice things. I had never seen her have the things any woman should have and enjoy. Our little blue convertible Mustang was filled, and we were ready to go. We said our goodbyes. I thought I could see a bit of concern on JM's face about leaving. I was happy but was already feeling a little sad leaving my mom, but we were off on our two-hour trip to a new life and job. We talked on the way down about things and life, hopes and dreams, and he took my hand and said, "As long as we are together, we can do anything, and with you by my side, I am the happiest man alive wherever I am."

We finally made it to the apartment, and Zack, who lived there, was waiting for us to arrive. He helped unpack our stuff and said to us that he worked just up the street about a block or so away, and that made me feel better because he would be close by if I needed him.

The apartment was huge, had big white column posts, just beautiful, and going into the living room, it had a very high twenty-foot ceiling and nice furniture. I loved it already. I was excited and a little scared at the same time. I had grown up fast with the fear of the unknown of what to expect from my brother Matt. So I knew I could do this and not be afraid in this big city. We had been married for about four months. We were still very much newlyweds, and the only people I knew was my brother, his wife, their beautiful little girl, and my aunt and uncle. They were all excited and happy we were there.

JM's new job started the next day. He had uniforms, and I didn't really know how to do laundry. I would usually take it to my mom's, and she would do it. So now I had to learn. We had to go to a laundromat and wash and dry our clothes, and I thought this was cool. I started looking forward to going in the evenings. He had to drive to work there, so I didn't have a car to drive. This made me feel a little uncomfortable as I had always had the car.

Zack stopped by the second morning. We were there to see how I was doing and brought a bag with a couple of glazed donuts and said he was just up the street if I needed him. He was such a great brother, and man, I loved him so much. I was just so happy to be here in this huge apartment, and my mom would call me every day, and my aunt Ethel would call and say she will come by and pick me up and take me to her house one day soon. I was excited; I loved her so much.

A few days later, she came by and went to her house. She fixed lunch for us, and I spent the day with her. She wanted my mom to come down and stay with her. My uncle was very sick, and she needed help with him. We had a great day, and she came often as she could, and we went out to the stores and got what she needed. My uncle's illness got worse, and she couldn't leave him to come and get me. This made me sad, and I missed her.

After a few weeks went by, I was getting bored and thought I needed a job or something to do but no way to get to or from because we didn't have but one car. JM could see something was wrong, and he asked his grandmother if we could buy her car so we could have a second one for him to drive to work, and I would have a car to drive if I needed it. She sold it to us, and we were thankful and glad she charged him five hundred dollars and then told him he could just have it, and we didn't have to pay for it. We were so grateful. JM always knew just what to do, and he was wonderful. Now I just had to figure out how to get to my aunt Ethel's house. That's the only place I was interested in going. The job though kind of faded out because I loved her so much, and now my mom was staying with her.

JM said, "I will show you how to go. We would drive over."

And I would drive back and forth until I could make it on my own. I would go almost every day. My uncle had gotten better, and my mom had to go stay with my sister Jean again for a while. We had such fun times; we would get a watermelon and go back to her house, cut it up, and eat the whole melon. There was no one else like her.

I loved her so much as I had great memories of her as a child. She would dress me up in pretty clothes and treat me like a little princess. She was the one who gave me the little red-beaded purse when I was in second grade.

She was married to an older man. They owned a big restaurant there but now was retired. He was not able to drive, but now I could help her, and soon my mom would have to come back down to stay with her. She was the one getting very sick now. She was losing a lot of weight and looking very pale. I was beginning to worry, and when she started to wear a wig, I asked my mom what was wrong with Aunt Ethel, and she was very quiet, and I did not know at the time that she had cancer. Later she told me she had bad cancer and would be getting worse. My heart was broken. She spoke to me a lot about her things and said she wanted my mom to have everything after she and my uncle passed, and I would tell her I didn't want to talk about it because it made me sad. My cousin Ella lived there also, and she loved my mom so much, and I didn't really know her but had seen her once or twice, and I thought she was so beautiful.

my cousin Ella

· She came by my aunt's one day when I was there. She had just gotten off work; she was a supervisor at the hospital there, drove a new car, and had her own apartment, and she had written a book about her life.

I knew I wanted to grow up and be just like her. She had long beautiful nails and wore miniskirts and high heels and red lipstick. Now this might not seem to be your hero-type lady, but she was mine. She was so classy, and I really didn't know what classy was back then, but I knew it was something she had that made me want to be and act as she did. I got to know her much better and loved her so much. I knew I was only eighteen and had years to keep growing, so I had plenty of time. She would come by pick me up and take me to lunch and talk to me about her life. We had fun times. But I was concerned about my aunt Ethel. I spent as much time as I could with her also. I was blessed to have her in my life.

I would keep going to visit my aunt, and I could see she was getting worse, and she would talk to me about life and things.

She would say to me, "Be a good wife, but your husband should be a better husband than you are a wife. He should love you more than you love him. A man should treat a woman like a queen."

I would tell her that he did treat me so good and that he loved me so very much, and she would laugh and say, "Yes, I can see that, and if I hadn't, he would have been gone by now."

She would go on to say I should think about going back to school, but if that's not an option, I needed to get a job and work hard to achieve a career in something. I was very shy and told her about my job in the photo lab, and she said that was good, and she was proud of me. I also told her about the babysitting job; she said that was good too.

She said all women, young and old, needed to have a purpose to be learning something new every day, and that idle time was not good for anyone. It was a complete waste of your life, she said.

One day, at our apartment, it was a nice day, and I decided I would walk up the street to get lunch. I was getting braver by the days. I left, and it was a straight walk to the little fast-food place on the corner. I got my food to go, and back down the street, I went. I was feeling grown-up and confident until I got back to the door of the apartment, and it was locked. I didn't have the key. We had lived there for a month, and I had not gotten locked out. What was I to do? I had no phone, I did not know any neighbors, and I started to cry, feeling scared, very scared. JM was at work, and I didn't know how to reach him.

Then I remember my brother worked up the street. He said just a straight walk, so I laid my lunch down and off I went. I was so scared, but I kept going, and there was his job site, but I had to cross a four-lane highway. I just knew I couldn't make it, and then a deep feeling came over me, and I raced across that highway. When he saw me, he looked concerned.

He could tell I had been crying, and he said, "What's wrong?"

I told him I locked myself out of the apartment, then he kind of grinned and said, "It will be okay. I will fix it," and told me to come on, getting in his car. I felt such a relief he could do anything. I thought he was the best brother ever.

We got back to the apartment, and he tried to raise a window but could not and tried to use something to open the door, and nothing would work. Fortunately, he had gone with my brother Robert to the landlord's house and knew where he lived. We went to get a spare key and to us disperse. The landlord was horrible and said it would cost us twenty dollars to use a spare key to get the door opened.

My brother was furious and said, "You must be kidding me."

The man said, "No, I am not, and she shouldn't be out if she doesn't know to take the key."

My brother jerked out twenty dollars and took the key and said, "He will bring it back shortly."

We got back, opened the door, and he said, "Get ready to be moving. I am going to find you another place." That guy made him so mad, but I was just thankful to get back in the house and thought I would not venture out like that again.

My brother came by one evening a couple of weeks after I had locked myself out and said he had found us a better apartment. The rent was about fifteen dollars higher on the month, but we needed to take it and leave, so we did, just like that. We lost our deposit because our six months was not up. We had only been there not quite three months, but we moved anyway. We packed up our car again and moved to a new apartment complex. It had a washer and dryer and was so very nice. We were very happy, but I was going to have to learn the new route to my aunt's house. This was not going to be as easy. My brother seemed to be very happy about our move. We were closer to him, and that made me happy.

I quickly learned the new route. My brother Robert came down to see my aunt, and he stayed with me. He was happy also with our new apartment; he had heard what happened with the landlord and the key.

I did not realize he was there seeing my aunt because she was dying of cancer. After he left, my mom stayed with her the remaining time, and I was glad because I could see them almost every day.

Summer was getting close, and my aunt was in and out of the doctor's office and the hospital. I was getting very scared, thinking this could take her life, and I could see the worry on my mom's face. I had always said to myself that I wanted to have my kids early in life. My mom was old, it seemed, when she had me and always felt like I had an old mom, and the other kids always had young full-of-life moms, and of course, she couldn't help it. She had ten kids, practically raising all of them by herself.

One day, I woke up sick to my stomach, felt like I was going to throw up, and I called my mom and told her I felt sick and maybe would not be able to visit them that day.

She immediately said, "Carolyn, you may be pregnant."

I said, "No, don't think so."

When JM got home, I told him, and we went straight out and got a test to check. It was positive. I was so happy and scared at the same time. I felt like I was still just a kid in the process of growing up and now going to have my very own baby. The first ones we called was my mom and aunt.

My aunt was very happy for me. She said, "You will be the best mom because you have so much love to give, and you will grow as your kids grow and learn life as you go."

My mom did not have much to say. I thought she had such a hard time in life. She was not ready for me to have kids.

My aunt was put in the hospital shortly after my news, and she stayed in for a few weeks. Lots of family came to see her, but I was just not accepting that she was leaving us. I wanted her to be here for a long time, and she was younger than my mom, so she should be as healthy as her. However, that was not the case, and I had to face the truth. She was going quickly, and I got to see her for the last time in the hospital, and she was so thin and frail. She was not my attractive aunt whom I looked up to as a little girl. This cancer had taken her life over.

She passed away, and my heart was broken. How I would miss her, no one would know.

I went to the funeral but did not look at her. My mom said it was bad luck to look at a corpse when you are pregnant, and it scared me, so I turned and did not look. I was glad I had seen her in the hospital; I wanted to remember her as the beautiful woman she was before cancer.

I always remembered her words and tried to live by them. She was strong and smart and much loved by me. We loved living in our new apartment, and after my aunt passed, I decided I wanted to get a job, and so I did. We had traded our little blue mustang off to a brand-new Mustang Mach 1 my brother signed for us because we had never had credit in our name, and we made him proud. We paid everything on time when or before it was due. We still had the little car Grandma had given us. I had got to drive a new car a time or two before but not our very own. We were so thankful.

Everyone was happy we were having a baby, and I had a good job working in a shoe store. The manager didn't mind that I was pregnant. It was very early, and I would be months before showing and could work for a while.

Since we didn't go home every weekend, my in-laws would come visit, and they were such good people and good family and so happy for us. We were always happy to see them; we missed them very much.

Zack said we would need to look for a little bigger place because we now had one bedroom, and said we would be growing out of this one.

I said, "But we like it here, and we think we can put a crib in our bedroom."

I knew he was thinking of something. JM was working hard and got a promotion already and an increase in pay. I felt very lucky and blessed, but my aunt's words would ring though, and I would think, yes, I was, but he was more so lucky and blessed to have me. But he knew that and would say it every day.

Now each day I would go to work, the manager would have me a glass of milk waiting, and I would tell him I did not like milk. He would say, "You may not like it, but that baby you are carrying loves milk, and so you must drink it," and I would. I hate milk.

Finally, I was so sick of the milk every morning, so I told him no more. It was making me sick, and I was not going to be able to work if he kept it up, so he said, "Okay, I will figure out something," and he did. The next day, there's no milk. I was so thankful, and the day went on and was a good day. However, the next morning, I came in, and he had hot chocolate waiting for me.

He said, "This is milk, and I know you can't say you don't like hot cocoa."

I said, "Well, maybe this might work. Why didn't you think of it in the first place?"

He laughed, and from then on, while I worked for him, that's how I got my milk intake. He was the best boss ever, and I had a great job that I enjoyed.

Working in that small shoe store helped me become less timid and shy and more outgoing and friendly.

One morning, as I was traveling through the neighborhood to get to work, it was lightly misting rain, and all at once, I lost control of my car and started sliding around. I was terrified of what was happening, and then my car landed in the front yard of someone's house. I was crying, and I didn't have a phone as cell phones were not available yet. A car came by and stopped to see if I was okay, and I told them I was pregnant and very scared. The man told me I had hit some black ice, and I was very lucky. He got the car out of the yard, and after a few minutes, I drove back to our house as I was very close and called my boss and told him what happened. He said he understood and that I didn't need to be out on the roads due to the ice.

I told JM what happened when he got home. He was just so glad I was okay. He said I should not work anymore due to the winter weather. It was coming quickly, and I should be home, taking care of myself. But I did not listen and continued working until I thought my baby was due within the month. We did not get a doctor in

Lexington because I thought I should be around family back home when the baby came, and that ended not being a good idea. I drove back in the mountains each month to get my checkup. The doctor said everything was fine and that I was doing great. I never felt bad at all. This seemed like an easy thing to do.

I wondered if this was all there was to have a baby; I was using it for sure. So far so good. While we were living at our cute little apartment, Lou let her girls spend the night with us. She was traveling somewhere at the time, and I had already set up a baby bed someone had gotten for me in the bedroom, so her youngest had grown up a bit since I had stayed with her. She was now about four years old, and the other one was about eight. They were such beautiful kids, and that four-year-old had my heart for sure. She was still small enough to sleep in that bed, but she refused. She wanted to sleep in the big bed, so both of them and me slept in the bed, and JM slept on the couch in the living room. I will always remember when I woke up the next morning, the four-year-old was looking at me straight in the eyes, a very solid look, no smile, no expression. I just reached over and pulled her up in my arms and told her that she was a doll, and if I had a little girl, I wanted her to be as beautiful as she was. About then, the eight-year-old said, "What about me?"

I replied, "You are a beauty too, young lady," and she was.

I enjoyed them so much and appreciated Lou for allowing them to stay with me. I only got them that weekend, and it was a fun time. My older brother Robert brought his son down to see a doctor for an illness he had, and he stayed over with us a couple of days. I remember one evening, we ate Arby's roast beef, and he said they were the best he had ever eaten. That made me glad because I got to share that with him. He had never eaten them he said. He was the one who helped us move here, and I was very thankful for him and would do anything for him. While he was there, he went and spent some time with my mom who was staying with my uncle and taking care of him.

My life was good. I was getting ready for my baby. I just knew this child would never have to feel like I had felt throughout my life. It would feel love. I sure had so much to give. I was ready, or I thought I was.

As my time got nearer, I got anxious. They put my uncle in a nursing home, and my mom went home. I was sad that she wasn't nearby in case I needed her. I went for my doctor's checkup, and he told me that I should be getting ready to come and stay close so I would be near the hospital when the baby decides to come. I had not thought about that and did not realize I would have to stay away from JM any at all. I guess I thought when I went into labor, I could get back in the mountains in time with no problem, but he advised not so.

I was so upset when I came out and told JM what we were going to do.

He said, "You will be fine. It won't be long, and we will work it out. Just don't be upset. Everything will be fine."

Oh Lord, it was not fine. What was I thinking when I decided to like this? How could I be so stupid? What was I going to do?

So the next two weeks went by, and March was upon us, and my due date was the sixth, so we packed up the things needed for the hospital and off we went back for me to stay with his parents until I had this baby, and you might be wondering why I was not staying with my mom. Well, the only reason was my brother Matt. He was still coming in and out, causing grief to my mom.

JM thought it was safer for me to be closer to the hospital. My mom did not have a car, and I would not have one while I was there either as I thought I would only be here a week max. Oh, how I was wrong and in for a shock of my life.

My in-laws were wonderful, good people, and they had raised a saint of a son. They lived across a swinging bridge that swung side to side when you walked on it. You had to walk very slowly to stay steady. I hated it. So many words cannot describe. So we made it, and I cried on the way and wiped my tears. I was an emotional wreck.

We made it and carried in my bag, and everyone was glad to see me. It seemed there were so many in that house, and here I was taking up a bed of the three bedrooms for the five people who lived there. So I thought this would be over soon with no problems.

Early Monday morning came, and no labor started so back to work. My husband had to go and left. I cried for him, and he said, "I will be back before you miss me," and he left crying too. The days were long. I talked to my mom every day. She was mad. I think because I wasn't over there with her, and I was too, but I knew to stay here was closer for me and safe. I was very shy and would not ask for anything to eat, and I would just eat whatever they had every morning. Breakfast, lunch, and then dinner, they drank sixteen ounces of Pepsi every day, and when they fixed lunch, I would have this huge drink set for me, and I got used to it and liked. I had not had sodas like that growing up ever. I guess we couldn't afford them. I thought my in-laws were very rich.

The week went by and nothing. Friday evening came, and my love came home. I was so happy to see him, and he would take me over to see my mom, and she said, "You could go anytime," and I said I thought I would have my baby this week, but I had two more days before the actual due date. We were hoping but nothing and no signs, so the weekend ended too quickly and off he had to go again. Oh, how sad I was. I would just go to the bedroom and cry.

Another week of the same routine, I thought, *Lord, please let it be this week.* Due date had passed, and my mother-in-law said, "You could go two weeks over with your first one. Most times, it's two weeks early."

Then I got worried, thinking something might be wrong, and I surely didn't need anything else to worry about. I was missing the love of my life so much and was so lonely. I needed him here with me, and he was working and could not be with me, and I knew there was nothing he could do. Another week went by, and now we were going into the third week. I went back to the doctor, and he said the baby was taking its time, but I was gaining too much weight. I had put on ten pounds in the two weeks. I had been there. I cried in the doctor's office, and he advised I needed to watch this closely. I had done really well with my weight gain during the first months, and this was not the time to be gaining weight. I went back hoping that weight meant that the baby was ready to come.

Someone should have helped me realize the steps of being pregnant; no one ever talked about it. My mother-in-law was going through menopause and was having a hard time. I didn't know what that was or meant, so I just was there. However, it must have been a worry to her as I was on my sixth week. It was now past March, and no baby. Had I made a mistake in the timing? No, not me. It must have been the doctor because he was the one who set the due date.

How was this happening to me? I was still just a teenager who did not know anything at all. *Lord, help me please.* There had been a tornado in Lexington. My love had to go through alone; it was an awful time. I was so worried. Everyone was worried. I was a month overdue with this baby. Something had to give here quickly. I had gained around fifty pounds in six weeks, eating Reese cups and drinking soda pop. Friday came, and I had my first pain. I was never so happy and glad in my life. I knew it was time we left for the hospital but got bad news.

The doctor came in and said, "It will be a few days."

I said, "How can this be? No, it has to be today."

"Go home and walk as much as possible. This will help speed up your labor."

So we did, and I cried. We walked, and we walked so far and so long. The pains got worse. So back we went, and finally he put me in the hospital in a room. I was huge, but I knew it was all going to go away shortly when my beautiful baby came. So I was in focus on getting this over and going back home with JM. Was I in for another surprise? First day came and went. Next day came, and in the third day, I had walked that hospital like five hundred miles. I was completely exhausted, not one ounce of energy left. What was wrong with me? Why was my baby not being born? I was extremely stressed, and I could see the concern and worry in his eyes as JM held my hand so gently.

He told the doctor he had taken off work, thinking we were going to have this baby three days ago, and he couldn't leave me and needed to be here, so the doctor broke my water, and I thought,

What was that? Could he have done that weeks or days ago? I was feeling a bit confused but too exhausted to think.

He said, "You will be a daddy soon," and off we went to the delivery room, and with pains, I pushed hard.

I heard the nurses say, "You have a beautiful baby girl," and she put her on my chest. I would always believe I fainted or passed out when I saw her. It was more joy than I could take. They did allow me some time to sleep and rest as I was totally exhausted. This had been so long and hard but well worth the pain when the nurse came in with my beautiful baby, and I gave her bottle and just cried and cried.

The nurse said, "You are very emotional."

I just nodded my head. I couldn't speak. Just looking at her was all I could do. This was a love I had never experienced, and I had heard people say love starts when you have your baby. Somehow I knew no one had ever felt like me, and no one but Jesus could love this baby more than me. She was red and puffy probably because she had refused to come out on time and stayed in an extra month.

Just in a few minutes, her daddy came around the door, and the love in his eyes was shining brightly between us. Now we light up the hospital. What an awesome, wonderful, blessed time. Our baby girl was here. His family came by that day to see me, and I would always remember his older sister saying that he didn't seem to be disappointed that I didn't have him a boy. I immediately said I wanted and wished for a baby girl and not once did I think I was having a boy, and he was the proudest daddy I had ever seen.

She didn't say any more about that; however, she did go out and buy a blue dress without me knowing I had not thought about the ride home before and didn't have anything, so we stayed three days, and if you could believe such a thing, his sister brought that outfit to the hospital, and that's all I had to dress her in to bring her home. I was humiliated mad and could have screamed loudly, but I was so happy that I was going home. I kept in my tears and wondered how rude to buy blue for a new baby girl but appreciated the gesture. JM didn't know until she came to help me get her dressed. As soon as we got back to his mother's house, I took it off her, and she never had that dress on again. My friends had dropped off gifts for her at the house, and she had so many cute things. I just kept dressing her up like a doll. We did get bad news. She had a little place on her right ear lobe that had to be removed and said they would schedule for me to bring her back by ending of her first week, and the doctor advised me to keep her at my in-laws for one week. I was devastated. How could this be happening? I just wanted to go home. I had worn the same clothes home from the hospital that I wore in because my pants wouldn't go up past my knees. Why had this weight not went away like I thought it would? I was huge. My baby weighed seven pounds and seven ounces. What was I going to do? I did not have big clothes. I wore a size ten to twelve. What had happened to my body? There was no time to think much about me now. I had another week to survive and get my baby where she and I belonged.

JM left, and we both cried. Little Michelle continued crying the entire week. I was torn badly and so sore and hurt so bad I cried, and she cried. Neither one could sleep, keeping the whole house of seven people up, I was sure. Three days went by and with no help from any of his family, not intentionally. I liked to hope, but I was very selfish with her, not wanting people to hold her and breathe all over her, and she was crying all the time. We missed our rock, and he would not be back until Friday night. I called the doctor as I did not think this was normal for a baby to cry all the time and sleep a little and wake up crying. I would sleep with her on my stomach and try and sing to her. Sometimes she would go out, and the other kids in the house would turn on loud music, and she would come crying.

Her doctor said she might have something called the colic that babies get and called her in some drops. They seemed to help just somewhat, but the crying did continue. I really didn't know who was the most miserable, she or me. Or we could have been a match. My pain was almost unbearable. No one told me to take an aspirin or something to help relieve, and of course, I didn't have a clue about anything again. I was not with my mom maybe. She could have helped me and know what to do. I had suffered deeply for six weeks and now another one, but somehow I knew if I could make another day and get this place, took off my baby's ear, and go home, life would be good.

Friday came. We took her at 5:00 p.m., and the place was removed. All went well, and in Saturday morning, we headed home. From that day on, she never cried much at all unless she wanted a bottle. She slept only, had to get up one time a night for a couple of weeks, and then she slept all night. I really believe we both knew where we needed to be and just cried until we got to our home. I had gained so much weight. I felt miserable but so happy with my baby girl. I tried to not think about. I was still very sore and would cry often when my baby was down for a nap. Why in the world did someone not tell me about something about this pain?

I was now nineteen and not a child anymore. I should never have to suffer pain like that. It was not mental pain; it was totally physical pain. My breasts filled with milk, and me again not knowing why, and what was happening, hurt worse than the other end. They were hard and firm and huge. They felt like they would burst, could not touch, and could not wear a bra. Again no one said I maybe should have breastfed my baby, but how was I to know this would happen? It really shows how family and friends are. I should have read books about having babies. I never knew what was involved and how much you need to know to go into this beautiful experience. My Lord had to be with me, or I was not sure I could have survived. Those first few months seemed like. The pain lasted forever, and to make things even worse, I got an enlarged cyst where I had been torn giving birth. Later my sister-in-law said if I had a good doctor, he would have cut me to keep from tearing. I had a lot of stitches and horrible pain from that, and with the cyst, it was almost unbearable. I had to sit in a hot bath as I could stand it twice a day. Finally by the grace of God, it busted on its own, and my bed was filled with the drainage. I felt that pain lifted from me. I thought to myself, *Why had I had such a hard time? Why did things happen like they did? Was I ready for a baby? Had I grown up too fast? Did I think I needed a baby to complete JM and me?* No one else I had known who had babies seem to have gone through anything, or did I just not know? But all

I knew was this baby girl had taken over my life and love. I could survive anything now.

When she was two weeks old, we moved from our cute apartment into a duplex right down the block from my brother Zack. He was thrilled, and so was I.

The landlord said we could make changes, paint, etc. and take it out of our rent, and boy, did I. The first thing I did was fix my baby's room with pink shag, thick shag, and pink paint. The landlord had someone come in and lay down the carpet. I love it. I told him I would paint, and he said, "You just had a baby."

I said, "That's okay. I want to do it myself."

Keep in mind, the pain was terrible and not going away, so I had to keep busy.

His wife called me and said, "Honey, you really shouldn't be doing anything for six months to a year after giving birth."

She didn't realize how excited and happy I was to have my baby where she belonged, and with the thrill of having her own room, I could do anything.

She said, "Honey, you need to talk to your mother about this."

She didn't know my mom had ten children with no doctor to deliver and no medicine to take that I heard of, so I was no powder puff. I had come from a strong woman, and I was ready.

When you are nineteen and had to grow up with no childhood to speak of, I was determined to make the home for my baby girl so she would feel like a little princess and never have to be left out and feel like I did when I was a child.

We didn't have much or any money. JM worked for a cola plant, and we made it okay. Our focus was on our baby girl. What a joy this was going to be going forward and how my life had changed. Was I ready? Yes, I was.

We got started on remodeling the apartment. School was out, so my brother-in-law Shane came down to stay for a while with us, and he was a great help. We painted and got our apartment fixed into a home, pink walls and pink shag carpet for my baby's room. That's all I wanted now. She was in a princess's room. It really looked so good, and we had the entire apartment looking like a showplace, and she was not yet a month old. She grew fast, and my weight was coming off very fast also, and I was feeling better and very happy. JM was working at the plant and had taken on a part-time job at Zach's service station in the evening until 9:00 p.m. He would go from his plant job straight to the service job, and I had worked hard also getting our things all organized.

It was time for baby's six-week checkup, and we had not been back home, so everyone was excited to see her and had gifts waiting for her. The doctor's visit went great. She had gained a couple of pounds and was beautiful. We could not have been happier. June was here, and it was summertime. Now life was good.

The baby was sleeping all night by now and was the best child we could have to ask or hope for. I was so in love. I was silly. I thought I was the only person who could feel this way. She had no hair around her little bald head, but I knew somehow she would have beautiful hair. I couldn't wait. I would try and stick little bows on her head, but they would fall off. I would dress her multiple times a day in different outfits and just look at her. She could smile now and laugh out loud. What more could I ever ask for? This child was a true gift from God. He had given me something to love and take care of.

Four months had passed, and I would sit her up on the couch, and she would roll over and laugh almost to losing her breath and still no sign of hair on her head.

JM and I had not had a honeymoon. We never thought about one. We just enjoyed every minute we could, and one evening, he said we should go somewhere on a short vacation. He knew I had worked hard and had a very stressful time having our baby and said it would help me, and of course, I could not even think about leaving this baby. She was my life now.

It was our second-year anniversary, so when Zach's wife said her sister-in-law, which was family, would keep Michelle for us, we decided to go. We went to Florida, drove straight down, and I cried most of the way.

John said, "Honey, you need this trip. You have done so much. You need the rest."

We stayed for two days and I wanted to come home and we did have a good time. I think he needed my attention on him because he was working two jobs providing for us, and we weren't getting the time we had before together. It was a fun trip but a short one. Everyone was shocked when we came back so early. JM and I spent the remaining time with Michelle for our second anniversary and were very thankful.

A couple more months passed, and there was a job opportunity came up at a local telephone company that paid well, and I was asked if I wanted the job, and I said, "No, I have an eight-month-old baby."

I spoke with JM, and he said, "Do what you want to do? It's up to you."

I spoke with Zach one day when he stopped by to see us as he lived just down the street. He advised me to take the job, and that it would be good for me, and his sister-in-law would babysit for me. I told him I wanted to just stay home with the baby. I couldn't leave her.

He said, "Well, you should give it a try and see if it works out for you."

JM was working two jobs, and we could use the money. Our rent was higher, and we had a new car payment, and Michelle's needs had increased. We had to depend on ourselves; we had no one to help us.

So, yes, I said to the job and started in December that year. It was cold and snowy winter, and I worked different shifts some days. I would drop off Michelle, and she cried a few times, and I would leave crying to work, but after a few days, she was fine and would wave bye at me, but it never got any better for me. I was a mess and would cry all the way to work.

Just as I got used to my job and working and liking what I was doing, my babysitter got sick and could no longer keep Michelle. I thought about how this could be. I was just at the point of not being a complete mess leaving this child because I knew she was well taken care of. What was I going to do next? There was another lady who was recommended highly to babysit, and now I had an almost one-year-old getting ready for a birthday party.

I went and checked out the lady and looked up to ask questions. She could see I was a young mom with concerns, and she understood and was polite.

We planned, and the next week, we had a new sitter. Michelle cried and cried, and I went on to work but felt horrible inside. I did not do a good job and asked if I could leave early, not feeling well. When I got there to pick her up, she was playing with another child. This lady was also keeping. I felt bad as the lady asked why I was there early, and that I still had to pay for a full day. I was young and thought nothing of it.

The next day, when dropping her off, she screamed very loudly and held tight to me. She was, indeed, very spoiled for me, and that was fine, but I left her and cried again all the way to work. I thought I was twenty years old, and I didn't think I would make it if this continued. I thought, *Lord, what I am going to do?*

JM could see the stress on me and would say, "The baby is fine. Don't worry. Everyone works and leaves their kids."

I called the next day and stayed home and decided I was not going back. That very evening, my boss called and said we were on a company strike, and there would be no work until further notice. This was true in my mind, another gift from God. I was so happy.

JM was as happy as me because I was home. The company called and asked if I could stand on the line at the local store a couple of hours a day, and I said, "Could I bring my little girl?" They said yes. Oh, how happy I was, and when they said to "bring a copy of your bills, we are going to help pay them while we are out," I couldn't believe it.

A full year passed, and our company stayed out on strike, and now this baby girl was two years old. My life could not have been better. She was with me every day. All the employees loved her. She could talk like an adult, sing for people, and was potty trained by fifteen months old. Yes, I was a proud momma. JM was a happy daddy, having his two girls home every night. He was still working two jobs every day, six days a week. He was the hardest working man everyone would say.

Good times were coming to an end. The company made a deal, and back to work, we were to go. I just couldn't do it. There was no way I was going to leave her now. JM came home from work that night. Michelle was in bed, and I told him about the news, and I was in tears.

He said, "I don't want you to worry. My dad has been talking to me about a job back home. It makes four times the money I am making here. This may be the time for us to think about moving back. You would never have to work."

I did not like that idea at all. What was he thinking?

I said, "No, there has to be another way."

Within two months, we were moved back home. Zach was very sad to see us leave, and so was I, but there was no other choice, or at least I didn't know of any. We looked at mobile homes to put in my mom's garden but didn't work out. Matt was still back and forth worrying my mom. Our aunt and uncle had an old house beside me, in-laws, across the swinging bridge for sale. It was in terrible shape, but everyone in JM's family said we could fix it up. It was cute. It was a two-bedroom house with a living room, kitchen, and small bathroom.

I was not afraid of a challenge, but this was a big one huge. The house had been rented out for years and had been empty for a couple of years.

My heart was broken to a point that I didn't know which way to turn. Should we buy this old house? Or should we try again and get a mobile home? I left it up to John to make the decision, and he said, "Let's buy the house and fix it up." So we did. What had I agreed to would hurt me deeply later.

My family was all disappointed that I had moved over beside my in-laws in this old house that needed so much work. However, it did not bother me because I could be home with my baby girl and enjoy every minute. JM would not have to work two jobs, and he would be with me and Michelle more.

First thing we did was have the old carpet taken out, and there were beautiful hardwood floors underneath that were redone and looked great. JM had started his new job and was leaving early and getting home early, so we loved spending our time together. Things were coming together, and our little home was looking wonderful, and I was adjusting but hated walking that swinging bridge, and that was the only way out at that time. I wondered how people could be okay with this. My mom lived out in the county, but at least there was a road to her house.

Zach came in for a visit to see me, and he asked, "How you could agree to live in a place like this after leaving your beautiful apartment?"

I replied and told him, "When I got this fixed up, it would be just as beautiful," and he just smiled at me.

We had several visitors, and I could see the looks on their faces, wondering why we were there. JM had grown up here and never thought anything of life here. It was normal, and I knew I could be happy anywhere I was with him.

Fall was passing, and winter was coming fast. My mom was still unhappy that I was there not knowing how I would react to being stuck with snow and ice. I really didn't think about it. I was busy working hard inside the house to make it our own. Wallpaper was really in style in the seventies, so I quickly learned how to use it and decorated the walls. I was pleased with my work. Michelle would be right by me, trying to help, and we would laugh. I would sit down, cuddle her in my arms, and tell her how much she was loved, and she would reply, "I love you, Mommy." That would put me back on my feet to work more. JM was busy making us a great living outside the house, and I was making us a great home inside the house.

When he came home from work in the evening, he would say, "Honey, you have worked too hard today. Who helped you?"

I would say, "Just me and my Michelle."

He would reply and say, "I don't like you doing this work yourself. Get someone to do it or at least help you."

He was so good at taking care of me and watching over me like I was a child, and that was okay.

We got our first snow in December. We were decorating for Christmas, and all was going pretty good until the day after Christmas,

December 26. We got a huge snowstorm, and the weather fell to zero degrees. Our water froze, and we had none the next morning.

I said, "What are we going to do? How long will it stay frozen?"

JM said, "Don't worry. It should only be a day." I wished he was right.

Three months passed, and the water froze solid. I had gotten depressed. Snow was on the ground the entire time that we could not get out due to the freezing cold and having to walk so far to get to our car parked on the other side of the road. There was one day that my mother-in-law watched Michelle until I walked over across the bridge to a lady's house, who baked beautiful birthday cakes and got one for JM's birthday and carried it back home. That's the only time I was out. My brother Robert offered to come to get us and bring us to Mom's for a few days, but I kept hoping the water would come back on. The neighbor who lived on the other side of the bridge had four sons, and they kept us from the water, bringing it every day. I honestly didn't think I would have made it without them. Every time I saw them, which was not often, I thanked them for all they did. By grace, they were there for us.

swinging bridge

Finally, the day came, and we had water. I felt like I had just become rich. I spent the whole day cleaning, doing laundry, and being grateful. Spring was just around the corner. We finally could get out, and straight over to my mom's, we went. She was so glad to see us. Her water had not been off one time. She did not like me living where I was, and she made it known to me and everyone else. The baby was going to be three years old in a few weeks. How time passed so quickly.

We went to church with my mother-in-law and JM's grandmother. They were good people, and we had a good Sunday school teacher for Michelle and one for us. JM and I accepted the Lord as our savior and was saved and baptized in the river. There was still some ice floating down the river as it took a very long time to go away. It was like warm water to us. However, as we were with other friends who also had accepted the Lord as their savior and they did two by two with two pastors doing the baptizes, we both went down together and came up as God's children.

Everyone was singing and rejoicing; it was a blessed day.

I was never depressed after that as I could turn to my Lord if I was having a bad day and knew there was nothing that he could not get me through. I knew I was not spending another winter across that river without a road. I did not know how I was going to change things, but I certainly was going to try. I did some research on who owned the property, going in behind the homes over there. Only four homes down the hill before you crossed the railroad tracks, but that was not an issue for me and none of my business.

I found out who owned the property, and everyone I asked about said, "You will get nowhere with this person. They will never agree to sell or let anyone come through that property."

I said, "I have nothing to lose, just going to try." I went to visit myself, and they were right. I didn't make any progress, so I left.

Later I thought everyone who knew JM loved him. He was the best man I had ever known, and surely he might make a difference. So after a couple of weeks went by, he and I went back to the house to plead with them to allow a road through their land. The lady invited us in, and we sat down, and we again told her how we had a terrible winter, and we had a three-year-old little girl, and we were going to have to move because we could not go through another winter.

Then she interrupted us and said, "Do you all own the house you live in?"

We said, "Yes."

She said, "I will think about it and let you know." She called within that week and said because and only because we were a young family over there, she would agree for the road to go through her land. I was so happy I called everyone I knew to let them know we were getting a road to our home. Everyone was so happy. My in-laws were shocked. They said they had been trying to get this done for fifty years, but I owe the glory to the Lord that she agreed.

By the next winter, the road was done. It took a long time to cut down the hill behind our house, but finally we had finished the road and the driveway in front of our house. Made a huge difference now back to what I was used to going out of the house, getting in my car, not having to walk down a long path, and getting on a long swinging bridge to get to the car. Life was good. I was thankful.

Our house was coming together, looking good. My mom was coming for more visits. It was hard for her to walk the bridge. She would stay a few days, and we liked that.

The road was very dark coming down the hill, and one day, we stopped at the service station in town to get gas, and one of the city officials owned the station, and when my girl and I went in to pay for the gas, the gentleman was in the store, and he asked me how we liked our new road. He knew JM, and I said, "We love it. The only problem is it is so dark coming down at night, kind of scary."

He said, "I will take care of that problem for you."

I said, "How can you do that?"

He said he would put a streetlight behind my house that would shine up and down the road, and he did that very week, and it made my week. I was again so happy and grateful for this kind of man.

The following winter wasn't so bad at all; water did not freeze once. The snow wasn't anything like the prior. I thought, *Wow, that first one must have been tested for us.* However, it made us stronger and more appreciative of what we had.

JM's grandmother lived just below us, and we loved her so much. She was such a good and kind woman. She only had two daughters, and they were blessed to have her we all were. Most times, when we would go visit my mom when she was home, Grandma would come out the door as we were pulling out the driveway and asked us where we were going. I would say, "Going to my mom's," and she would say, "Let me get my stocking and shoes on, and I will go with you." So we had to pull back down and wait on her, and she loved to go with us. I was happy she just had to come out her door and cross the yard to get in the car, no more walking that long bridge.

This, however, became a habit, and every time we would go anywhere, she wanted to know where we were going, and most times, she would end up coming with us. Thank God for those memories, and they continued up to her death.

Michelle had turned four and then five. We were having the best times a mommy and child could have, playing with my friends, and they had kids with the same age who would come up and play with her. Kindergarten was coming up, and she was excited. I wasn't. It seemed five years had flown by, and she had been begging for a little sister or brother. She said she would take either one, but she really wanted a sister. I had planned on another baby but was in doubt that I could love another child as much as her. When school started, she only went half a day, and I loved that knowing I would pick her up early just gave me more joy than anything else.

Fall came, and our second baby was planned just like the first, and we knew it wouldn't be long. Sure enough, the test came back positive, and another was on the way. I could not have asked for a better man to be married to and be on our journey through life. He treated me like I was his top priority, always attentive, and the most loving anyone could hope for. Our love was like no other I had seen or experienced. We were all very excited, and my little girl would be six years old and in first grade when baby number two came along.

I had a much better pregnancy because I had no stress having to leave my home. All was good. I only gained about thirty pounds, but in five years, my weight was not back to original and never would be. My entire body had changed completely. However, I knew much better how to take care of myself. Time went quickly, and again I was due in late April, not sure why my babies want to take so long to come down the birth canal but ended in mid-May for baby number two. How happy and blessed was I, and JM was, I think, more excited than me because we did this together the entire time, no time apart.

I felt like my family was complete now and was ready to see what the future would hold for us.

Having the opportunity to be a stay-at-home mom for both of my girls was such a blessing that even I at that time did not realize. JM worked every day, and he got and put on the second shift at work. For a while, he was working from 2:00 p.m. to 11:00 p.m. We did not like that. When it was time for Michelle to start back to school, she was in first grade. It was hard for him to be up when she went to school, and he was gone when she got home.

my brothers Robert and Zack

This, only by the grace of God, lasted a couple more months, and he was on the days getting home by 4:00 p.m. every day. Carol

117

was growing by the months, and we all could not have been happier. We would go to my mom's about every day. Zack and Robert loved my girls like their own. Zack had Michelle. They were crazy about each other from day one, and Carol had Robert from day one. I was happy because they loved them so much. Robert would take Carol home with him. He lived about a quarter of a mile up the road from my mom, and Zack lived right in the backyard, so both were very close. When we pulled up in the driveway, Michelle would jump out and run straight to his house. She also loved her cousin, Lilly Zack's little beauty. She was now about thirteen, and Michelle just adored her.

When Carol turned one year old, we took our vacation to Smoky Mountains and had a great time. She was walking and no longer took a bottle, and that was good.

Carol was a curly-haired beauty, and Michelle was growing up, now eight years old. My love and attachment to her was so different than any other mom. I knew she was the best child you could hope for. My mom would always say she was too good for her own good.

I would say, "Mommy, I don't know what that means."

She would say she was like an angel out of heaven, and I did agree with that.

A day came, and I will never forget that on a cold February day, we got the worst news that my niece Cynthia had passed away overseas. She and I were closer than sisters, and she had just been at our house during the holidays a couple of months prior. My heart was completely broken. I was in shock. How could something like this happen to a twenty-two-year-old beautiful girl? She had heart failure.

I dreamed about her after I had heard the news, and her parents were in the process of getting her body returned to the US. The dream was that I was at her funeral, and looking down at her, she rose up to me and spoke. When we got to the funeral home the next week, I knew how she was going to look. As I walked up with JM holding tightly to his hand, I looked at her, and it was exactly like my dream. She lay there with a slight bruise where she had fallen, and I felt faint as I knew we had spoken earlier. I had thought about that through the years and still could not understand how and why that happened, maybe because there was a strong love between us, and I treasured every moment we played together as children, and every moment we traded clothes and shoes and enjoyed every minute we had together. I was blessed to have had her.

A month later, we got the news that my sister-in-law had passed away, and we were all sad and left to go to the funeral. Zach drove my car. JM stayed home with the girls as we had a long drive picking up my sisters on the way.

We drove to Jean's house and spent the night. It was Zach, my mom, and me. I was up very early the next morning, coming into the kitchen, and Zack was sitting there all flushed and seemed to be in a lot of pain.

I asked, "How you are doing?"

He replied, "Not well at all."

I knew he had been on high blood pressure medicine and asked if he needed to take something or what I could do. He said he had been off the medicine for almost a year. I got really scared and asked him if I should take him to the hospital, and he said he would be fine, just maybe needed me to drive over to Ohio to pick up Ally and Lou. I told him I had not driven other than a couple of routes in Lexington, and he said he would be with me, and I would be fine.

Jean and my mom came in and could tell he was not feeling well. He was ready to go, so I drove, and he sat in front seat with me, and we finally made it after about three hours to Ally's house, and she and Lou were ready to go. I went in and told them what had happened, and I was scared to go on to the funeral. By this time, he seemed like he was fine and said he could drive, but Lou told him she would drive for a while, and she did. There were four of us in the back seat and two in the front. We finally made it, and my mom was trying to tell them how to drive and get there. She was about to drive us all crazy. We knew she had never been in this state before, so how did she think she knew the way?

We would all laugh until we were crying. Zack would say it's a shame for a family to be going to a funeral and laugh like this, and we would laugh again.

We finally made it and was a very sad time. I really loved my sister-in-law. She was the one who tried to get me to come and live with them when I was fourteen, and my mom wanted me to marry Lynn, so it was another difficult time for me as I was still fresh with the funeral of my niece passing the month before.

Soon we were on our way home. It was very late at night, around midnight, when I dropped Zack off at his house, my mom went home with me as she did not want to go into her house at midnight. I was happy she was with me.

A couple of weeks went by, and we were all recouping from the family losses. The kids and I went over to visit with my mom on Saturday, and Michelle jumped out of the car and ran over to Zack's. He had his yard all torn up, putting some line in, and as we were going in the door, I yelled and said, "What are you doing?"

He said he was working trying to get a waterline in, and it looked like he had a lot of help since several guys were helping. I yelled back and told him not to work too hard. We visited a long time that day, and later in the evening, we left going home. As I was leaving, I went to the end of the yard, and we spoke a few words. He said he was calling it a day. It looked like they got a lot done that day. Told him I would see him later, and the girls were hollowing bye to him, and they loved him, and I knew the love he had for them was priceless. He had always watched out for me, and I was grateful.

We got home, and later that night, my phone rang, and my heart sank with the news that Zack had died instantly with a heart attack. I thought, *Lord, this can't be.* I had dreamed after we got back from the funeral that my car was covered with muddy water. I never thought much about it as we had come from a funeral, and Zack had talked on the way home about people and families who did not need to be out so much and expense for fancy coffins and flowers, and that he didn't want any of that, and I said, "I'm not listening to stuff like that," as I didn't need to hear it. He would laugh and say he was just saying. How was I now going to make it without him? He had been my rock all through the years. I had just lost the third family member, and two of them were my closest at that time.

I could only think about my mom. Oh, how could she handle this? I took my heart and thought of her. Yes, he was my best brother, but he was her son. I put my feelings aside and just prayed she could get through this loss of a son. Oh, how she cried and cried. He meant so much to her just living in her backyard. But only if we knew what was around the horizon. God, help our family. We woke up to deep snow, and it was so cold. How could this be in April close to Easter time? Such a bad time for a funeral, the saddest I had ever felt, but I kept thinking about Mom. *Lord, just help her.* My family was so sad having to bury him in the snow-covered ground. It was almost unbearable. I had just seen him. I thought, *What else should I have said? What could I have done? Oh, how I miss him already. How did I know that was the last time I would see him?*

It's like time stood still for a while. I could not get my mind to accept what had happened over the past three months. No one in our family had died since my dad. Now Cynthia, who was more than a sister to me, was gone, and the best brother I could have ever hoped for, who always had my back, and was there for me was gone. My kind sister-in-law was gone. Michelle was having a hard time as she was very close to Zack, and Carol was only two but knew something was terribly wrong. Both had their quiet time with me. A few months went by, and I was going to Mom's daily, bringing her home with me, and trying to comfort her in any way I could. My brother Robert lived on up the hollow, and he was in grief as he and Zack were very close. Remember they were the ones together who moved JM and me when we were newlyweds, getting us started in life.

My heart aches for him, and I took Carol every chance I had to see him as she always brought a smile to his face. He loved her so much. He had bought one hundred or more little chickens and had them in a pin and called me and told me to bring the kids. He had them a big surprise. As I was driving up the hollow and passing by Zack's house, I teared up and tried not to show to the girls. As we pulled down his driveway, he was waiting on us with a big grin on his face. We got out, and he said, "Come on!" He took us to the caged pin, and there were so many little doodles. The girls went crazy, especially Carol, jumping up and down and screaming with joy. She had never seen anything like this, and it more than made his day. I just kept watching him as he would pick one up and have them hold it. I never liked chickens, so I stayed clear of holding one, and he got an even bigger kick out of that. We ended up bringing two of those things home with us, one for each, and he really wanted me one for myself, and I said, "No, thanks." He laughed.

A couple of days later, he called and asked if JM and I knew how to pick beans, and I said I had never picked a bean and asked why.

He said, "Come over this evening and help me get some beans picked."

I said okay. We left when JM got home from work, and I left the girls with Mom. Robert had the biggest garden I had ever seen, and he was always giving us stuff like tomatoes and cucumbers that I loved, so we were so happy to help him out.

There were so many green beans. I thought it would take forever, but we picked and got buckets full and talked and laughed the entire time. It was getting close to dark as the sun had gone down, and suddenly I felt a little scared, and about that time, something grabbed my ankle, and Robert yelled, "Snake!" I screamed so loud the entire hollow must have had me and ran as fast as I could out of that garden to the road. My heart was pounding so fast I felt like passing out. JM and Robert were standing there, bent over, laughing. There never was a snake. Robert had grabbed my ankle to scare me, and he sure did. I told him no more help with his beans by me.

I was so relieved not to be bitten by a snake. We all ended up laughing and going for ice cream. He did not let me live it down and told everyone we saw how he got me. He was such a jolly good soul. JM had been hunting and had sent him some game meat he loved. I called Robert the day before and said I would bring to him. He was thrilled as he did not hunt but love to eat the wild meat. I went over the next evening and waited, and it was getting very late at Mom's. He must have had to work late, she said. Thinking if I should take this on to his house or just leave here, and he could pick it up, but I really I wanted to see him, and so did the girls. He looked so forward to us, coming over although he would stop by our house on his way home at least once a week or more. Not thrilled about driving those roads after dark, we left, not having a clue on what was about to take place in our lives again.

I had another very strange dream a few weeks prior, and it was like I lived through losing another brother. In the dream, JM had come home from work, and I met him screaming at the door, saying, "I have lost my second brother." I remember waking up in a cold sweat and panic. I felt sure I was sobbing and mourning the loss of someone else and figured it was where stress and missing Zack was still affecting my sleep.

Later that night, after returning home, I did not see Robert as he must have had to work late. He worked so hard every day, putting in long hours. He was such a good man. The phone rang, and it was my mom. It was about midnight. She was crying very hard and told me Robert had died with a heart attack, and my thoughts went directly to my dream. It had come true. Maybe it was to prepare me so I could help my mom. She lived alone, and I felt should not have gotten news like this at midnight, I was furious and heartbroken at the same time. This was surely too much for any mother to take.

The next morning at daybreak, I was on my way to try and find out news on what had happened. The story went like he got home late, and his arms were hurting him bad, and he was taken to the hospital and passed away halfway there. It was like another nightmare and praying someone would wake us up soon. How could this be happening in our family of ten? Now we were a family of eight. We told Michelle but kept the news from Carol. She was two years old and would not understand.

The funeral came, and he was buried in the family cemetery, and how sad we were. Nothing could help me to grasp any of this.

Now my second-best closest brother was gone. How was I going to be okay? But then I thought how a mother could survive and be okay losing two of her sons within a six-month period. That would again be my focus to help in any and every way to shed hope to all my family. My heart was broken.

Each day, after taking Michelle to school, Carol and I would head to Mom's house. She was so sad. I just wanted to cry myself but knew I could not. I had to be strong. Sometimes we would go out to eat and shop, but nothing seemed to help her. She had that look in her eyes that was unbearable to stare into.

As time went by, there was some conflict in the family. Everyone was upset and seemed to be not themselves.

Carol started asking about Robert why he wasn't coming to see her, and with a broken heart, we told her he had gone to heaven, and that he loved her very much. It was a sad and heartbreaking time for us, but somehow, I knew we would get through this.

My baby girl Carol was growing, and so was Michelle. We went to Disney World the following year, and they had a great time and spent some time also on the beach. However, my mind still was not allowing me to accept losing my niece and my brothers, the three people who were the closest to me.

JM was very hurt with the loss of Robert and Zack. They were close, hunting together, going to shooting matches, and having times just to talk and have fun.

mom showing a quilt she made for me

Such a sad difficult time for the entire family. How does one adjust and cope with a tragedy like this? You just pray.

Time seemed to go slowly by. However, it was going very fast. We did some travel every chance we would get away, taking Mom with us to visit her daughters, and that helped. The conflict in our family got worse over time, bringing brother and sister against each other for no reason. In my opinion, I always tried to be the peacemaker in the family. I never liked to see them argue, and it was not good for Mom.

This continued and got much worse over time. Mom had always been afraid to stay by herself. Even when I was home, she never liked being by herself, so she would come to stay with me few days at a time, and I would be sad when I took her home, knowing how she felt. She was always ready to go anywhere I could take her.

She had told me when she was very young with a one-year-old child, she lived up a long hollow with no houses nearby. Being alone, she did not realize it was Halloween, and some family members dressed up and banged on her door. Upon opening, she was so scared she passed out, and the family members helped her regain consciousness, and she was so angry. She told them never to come back to her house again. When I heard this story, it made sense to me why she was so afraid. My heart had always felt heavy for her due to the life I had seen so far growing up and now being a mom myself. I often wondered why she chose to live that way and asked her once why she had so many children, and it seemed to make a much harder life for her not having a husband around to help. Her reply was that her kids were all that brought her happiness in life, and that's all she said about it. I did not ask any further questions.

I was blessed to have been raised by such a strong woman. My strength all came from her and her alone.

At this time, losing two sons, a granddaughter, and daughter-in-law within eight months showed her strength beyond words.

Ally was another strong woman dealing with the loss of her oldest daughter and two brothers. My heart was so sad for her as she was in a much difficult time.

She had a fondest for Carol, and we talked every day. She would call me, or I would call her. That helped her and me also. We planned a trip to the Mammoth Cave. She, the girls and I went and stayed in a hotel for a few days and had the best time. Carol investigated a bird's nest and got stung with a wasp on the chin. Ally immediately knew what to do for the sting, and our day went on as planned. We got lost, and I had to stop for directions as there was no GPS in those days. When the man was giving us directions, she got so ticked she had to get in the car. When he was done, I got in the car, and she was still laughing, and she asked how we were to go, and I started laughing and said I had no idea. We finally ended up on the right road and laughed, which was good for her at the time. Those were memories that will last me throughout life. She was a wonderful sister who was loved very much.

She would come to stay with my mom for a week or more at a time every vacation she got, and her time there was enjoyed by all of us.

JM's grandmother was now in her eighties, and a precious soul was she. Staying with his mom was beginning to show some wear and tear on both of their health, and his aunt was not able to have her stay with her. So when she asked JM about staying with us for a couple of weeks, we did not have any problem. I felt blessed to have her in our home. She did love us and was happy there, but her health was getting worse. She was not sleeping well at night, and I could not leave her alone during the day, but that was okay. We wanted to make her happy.

JM's mom came over and advised us that she and her sister had to put her in a nursing home due to her condition, and she did not want to go. We advised that she could stay with us awhile longer. They had made up their mind on what was best, and it was a sad time. Carol and I would go visit every day and take her a piece of Bailey pie that she loved so much. She would always ask when she was getting to come home, and my reply would be, "Soon, I hope." Three months later, she passed away, not being my grandmother. She was just as special to me as she was to anyone. I had not known my grandmothers, and she was all I had. It was a sad difficult time for JM and his family and the kids I had to be strong for them.

my brother Matt, mom and Jean

The local grocery had a part-time opening for a cashier, and I asked JM. He thought it was a good idea for me to do something like this part-time job in the evenings that they had asked me and really needed the help, and he could be home with the kids, and he said that sounded good, and I should try it.

That week, they called me every day, and I worked from about 5:00 p.m. to 9:00 p.m. I loved it, and I had the opportunity to see people I had not seen in years.

This seemed to help me as I was struggling hard with the loss of our grandmother and was still in mourning over my brothers.

Then one evening at about 8:00 p.m. on a cold October night, the manager said I had a long-distance emergency call, so I left my register and went to the phone, not expecting what I was about to hear. Ally was on the phone and said Matt had passed in his sleep, and she wanted me to go and let our mom know. She would not call her on phone and tell her this awful news. I was in shock as three weeks earlier, we were at my niece Misty's wedding, and he was doing so well. He had gotten saved and was in church. I was so proud of him. We had a great talk during the wedding's after-party, and in the morning, we left to come home, and again I thought, *How this could be happening in our family?* I still didn't remember hanging up the phone and driving to my house and telling JM what happened.

The next thing I knew, we were pulling in the driveway at Mom's, got out, and went in. By now, it was going on 10:00 p.m., and Mom said, "Honey, what are you all doing coming over here this late?"

And JM took my hand, and I took hers and said, "We have some bad news."

Everyone knew, as bad as Matt did, he was her baby boy, and she would have given her life for him. When we told her the news, that grief in her face and eyes would remain with me forever as the news of her third son had died at the young age of thirty-three years old.

She sat down and said, "How am I going to live without my boys?"

In the meantime, Ally had got the news from the rest of our family. Mom asked what happened to him, and I said he passed in his sleep peacefully. She also had a great visit with him at the wedding, getting good pictures, and seeing him sober was such a comfort to all of us. All the years, I had suffered from his ways, of his being an alcoholic. When he was sober, he was a great brother and son. He and Zack were the best when I was little, watching after me at school, and up until our father passed away, he was not any trouble at all. My thoughts were still he could not accept Zack leaving and our father passing all within a very short period, and he was deeply affected in a negative way.

He too was gone now, and there was seven. I was thinking how a mom would survive this tragedy in her family. Somehow, I thought this had been the worst I had seen her, and maybe where it had been three years since the others had passed, I wouldn't leave her. We took her back home with us that night to watch after her. The next few days were horrible with grief from everyone in the family, and another time that will be with me forever.

My focus again was to get my mom through this. Just when I thought she might live from losing two other sons, I now had to start all over, a mom and her three sons. The funeral was so sad. It was like everyone was numb with grief in our family. The neighbors and relatives were so concerned about our mother. She was a strong woman, and I felt she could get through it if anyone could.

Time went fast and turned around. I had a kindergartner ready for school. She cried and cried and said she was not going to school. I told her it would be fun and only be for half a day. This was another hard time for me as Carol was independent but was not showing when it came to school. I would leave her screaming and holding on to me so tight. I would be so stressed and upset that I would cry until I picked her up, and then she was fine. The teacher said she had a great day. This went on every day. She did not like her teacher, so I thought about checking on another school and was not happy with any that I looked at. JM told me to find something to do while she was in school to occupy my time, or I was going to be sick. I enrolled in the technical college for morning classes and started immediately. She still cried and screamed, but I told her I had to go to school too; this did help much.

I would cry all the way to the college and be all red-faced and red-eyed when I got there. I would just say I left my baby girl crying and holding on to me for dear life and was the hardest thing in my life right now to leave her. They would tell me that it would get better, but right now was what I was dealing with. She was such a good little girl; she just wanted her mommy. I must listen when Michelle would say, "Mom, we are going to have trouble with her." That would always make me laugh. I enjoyed my classes and ended up with a business and office degree that proved to help me later.

As quickly as school started, it was almost over, and it had certainly been a difficult year with her crying until the last day. I sure was glad when I picked her up on that last day. I was pretty sure that the kindergarten teacher was happy also. I figured none of the first-grade teachers would want her in class for the next year. They would all shut their doors and their classrooms to keep out the sound of her crying.

Summer was wonderful. She had turn six, and Michelle had turned twelve, and I was the proudest and happy mother in the universe. My girls and JM were my life, and I knew I could get through anything with them.

We stayed in the pool and went to the beach, just playing all summer. However, as fast as it came, it ended, and we were getting ready for fall school to start again. Carol already saying she was never going back to that school again. I advised she would have a different teacher, and she would love it. Michelle was going into seventh grade, and no one could have asked for a better child. She was a perfect child in my eyes. Carol had a deep attachment to me and didn't want me out of her sight for a minute. I would take them over to spend the night with my mom as she loved them so much. I had wished many times that she had loved me the way she did my two girls. They were her favorites for sure, especially Michelle. She would always talk about what a good child she was and wanted them to come often to stay with her. I would leave Carol crying for me not to go, but I knew at some point, she had to stop this, and after I left, she was fine.

The first day of school came around, and what I was afraid of happened. Michelle went straight on into her class as usual, and Carol clung to me and cried.

Technical college was finished. Now she would be going to school all day. This was going to be worse than last year. I cried all the way home and was stressed all day until it was time to pick them up. First thing Carol said was she had quit and was not going back. Michelle said she had a great day. JM advised me I was going to drive myself crazy doing this every day, and that I should do something to keep me occupied. So a few of the other moms and me started walking at the track every morning, and that helped, but she still cried and hung on to me as I had to leave her was almost too hard to bear for me.

A new teacher came in, and we had her switched, and that's all it took. She became much more satisfied and would still cry but not the same as before. I was thrilled for her and me. I was so thankful for this teacher, and many times, I would tell her so.

Then just as she was beginning to like the first grade, she got so sick. She would lay down wherever she was and go to sleep. I took her to the doctor, and he couldn't find anything wrong and said she might be going through a growth spurt. However, she kept getting worse, and I was very worried and took her back. He ran some tests and diagnosed her with mono. He said it was a severe case; she ended up missing thirty days of school, and we had prayer cloths under her pillow as she seemed lifeless. We had never been so scared in our life. Finally, she was okay. And back in school, the principal said if she wasn't so smart, he would have had to keep her in first grade for missing more than the allowed days. We were very happy. It would have been hard to do the first grade over with her.

Holidays came and went, and another year was over now. My big girl would be going into eighth grade. How could this be? It seemed like yesterday she was just beginning to walk.

Living by my in-laws was not easy, and our house needed a lot of work, but JM would not talk about moving. I guess he wanted his kids to grow up where he did. I did have wonderful in-laws, and they were such good people. However, it was hard for anyone to live so close to their parents, and it should not be allowed to happen. It takes up a good part of your life and energy just to try to get along with everyone. I felt guilty when I would go to Mom's and not ask if anyone wanted to go. My mom was alone and loved when I took the girls for a visit.

Sometimes I would get home about the same time as JM when the kids were not in school, and my mother-in-law would say to me that when she was young, she would always be home and have her husband a good dinner on the table when he got home from work. I would say, "That is good, and your mom lives right beside you. Mine don't, so I go see her every day, and I don't like to cook."

Usually, Mom would send our dinner home with me or come over and cook it for me.

We would all go on summer vacations together and, most of the time, have lots of fun. We split the costs, which helped us as I did not work at the time. I felt blessed to be home, but later I did go back to the part-time work at the grocery as a cashier when they needed me, and that seemed like every evening or sometimes during the day, and I would say no if I didn't want to work at that time, and it was okay because it was my choice. A lady approached me and asked if I would be interested in selling Avon.

I said, "No, thanks. Don't think so."

She said, "You would be so good at it and make extra money." She talked me into the job and ordered my stuff to get me started.

Later I became very good, had some regular people, made sales too, but got tired of deliveries taking up too much of my time, and handed it off to someone else and appreciated the experience.

Summer was coming to an end, and another school year was about to start second grade and eighth grade and as fast as that came, it went. Carol settled down and did not cry once. However, another little girl cried every day that year. I felt bad for that mom because I knew the feeling. Thankful that I did not have to go through that again was an understatement.

Michelle had to do some extra work dissecting a fish and a frog. I helped her, of course, and was happy she didn't mind the school workload, getting ready for high school. Her eighth-grade dance came up, and she looked as beautiful as a princess and had a cute little boyfriend. From her kindergarten graduation to her eighth grade, it just went by too fast. Carol had worn the same little dress for her kindergarten graduation as Michelle. I still had the dress in our closet.

Michelle had a couple of teachers in school whom I was unhappy with and let them know about it. I was reminded of a few teachers like that for me and wondered why some people chose that career if they were not good with kids, some maybe not even liking kids. However, ending year, Michelle came out with good grades and was thankful she had done a great job.

JM was working hard every day, making sure we had everything we needed and more. He was so good to me always, called me his baby, and would tell everyone he had three girls. He would sometimes go on a fishing trip with his parents or brother, and the girls and I would cry after him. We had done this for years. He did have us all spoiled.

JM had a really good job and got off work now every day at 2:00 p.m. He had just bought his dad's truck and was very pleased as this was his first truck and got it at the low cost of $3,000.

He had worked the second shift when Carol was a baby and took Michelle to school about every day until I was able to get out. If he wasn't up, she would walk down with some of the other kids and ride the bus. I felt our life was perfect, and our love was like no other I had ever seen or been around.

It seemed like time was going so fast. How could I slow it down?

When you are young, time is not supposed to go this fast. We turned around, and another year had gone. Michelle was in cheerleading now, going into high school, and Carol was playing ball. The girls were enjoying the school day.

Working one afternoon as a cashier, I had regulars come in about every day I worked, and a business gentleman came through my line and asked me if I would be interested in an office job, working full-time, and I really didn't know what to say. I wasn't sure, and it caught me off guard. I went home and told JM about it, and he said the girls were old enough and would be fine next to his mom's as we lived in thirty-feet-yard length.

I asked the girls and told them it would be during the day, and I would be home at 5:00 p.m. every day, and Carol said, "Who will pick us up from school?" And I knew it would be me.

I thought more about it, and a few days later, I went down and got the job. I couldn't believe it. I only had a high school diploma, and I did get the technical college degree that helped me get the job. It was a great big office with thirteen employees, and I was given the job of filing for the first month. I had never filed before, and it went very slowly. After that, I was given a desk job where I did checklists in a department.

The girls were adjusting to me, being a little late getting home, but when I took the job, my request was that I take lunch from three to four to pick up my kids, and they said that was okay, and I didn't have to use my lunch hour I could do during a break. However, I advised I just would do lunch so I could spend the time and only have to leave them for an hour when I got back. It all worked out fine.

Michelle was fourteen, and Carol was eight years old, and both were beyond their years. I was so proud of them, and the love I had for our girls was like no other I felt in the world. No one else could love their kids like me, or that was how I thought. I was making money, and my girls were doing great, and I was feeling pretty good. I got a promotion in three months, and an increase in pay made me feel like I was doing a good job. I was grateful to have a good job.

Mom and Jean

My mom had been worrying over Jean. She had been sick, so we went up for a visit one weekend, and she did look a little tired and lost some weight and said she had felt week for a while trying to get her strength back.

Later that summer, she came down for a visit with Mom along with our oldest brother Frank. They were very close to each other. The girls and I went over to see her, and she was lying down and taking a nap. Mom said she was tired, and we waited until she got up, and she looked very frail and thinner than she was when we visited earlier in the spring.

I could tell Mom was concerned but didn't say anything. Later that fall in November, she was diagnosed with cancer and given a few weeks to live. This crushed the rest of the family, and my mom was determined that she could make her well if she could get her to eat, but of course, Jean could not hold food down on her stomach. We could not believe this was happening. She had a husband and five kids and had worked so hard to have a good home and raised them to be good people, and her baby boy had just gotten married, and she had two beautiful little granddaughters to love and help show them the way. How was her family going to be okay without her? And more, how was her mom going to cope with this after the loss of her three sons? It already just didn't make any sense. I thought she was so strong and fierce. Nothing like this could happen to a wonderful woman like her.

It wasn't long before Christmas, her time came, and she passed away with her family all around her. After that day, my mom was never the same. She had now lost her firstborn child she had so long ago. When she was young and went five years before having the second child, they had a bond that was unbroken, and now she was gone. My heart ached so badly for everyone. Jean was so close to her kids. My heart was broken for them and my mom. The funeral was on a snowy icy day, the day before Christmas Eve.

Now our family was down to six from ten. There were two sons left and three daughters and the sadness in Mom's face, and eyes would make you cry, and I did. What a hard life she had and now giving up her firstborn child she loved. This time, I was not sure how effective I could be helping her make it through this terrible time, but I was going to give it my all because she was my mother who had raised me in ways I didn't understand sometimes but out of respect and gratitude to her for being the strongest woman I had known, and hopefully I could only hope to grow into that kind of strength in my lifetime by God's grace.

About the Author

Carolyn Whitaker Collett was born in Hazard, Kentucky, in a large family where there seemed to be no hope of success. She was determined that there was something more out there for her. She struggled as a child with little or no attention from her family and was bullied by other kids throughout every year of school. Working through hardships, she met the love of her life and was married at seventeen years of age, and anxious to begin a life long journey with her husband that would lead to having two beautiful daughters.

She worked hard to be the best mom, showing as much love as possible to her family. Started her career at a large company, working her way to the vice president position. She has never asked for a promotion or increase in pay; her work ethics were enough for the company to see her worth.

She decided to leave the company after twenty-eight years of service due to personal reasons and is very happy and grateful to all the people who helped her in life and career.